Ayr United - The Oddest Matches

Also by Duncan Carmichael:

Official History of Ayr United Football Club Volume 1,
Contour Press, 1990.
Official History of Ayr United Football Club Volume 2,
Contour Press, 1992.
Images of Sport Ayr United FC, *Tempus, 2001.*
Ayr United Classics, *Tempus, 2002.*
100 Ayr United Greats, *Tempus, 2004.*
Walking Down the Somerset Road, *Fort Publishing, 2006.*
Ayr United Miscellany, *Amberley, 2011.*
Ayr United At War, *Mansion Field, 2014.*
Ayr United On This Day, *Kennedy & Boyd, 2016.*
Ayr United FC Managers, *Kennedy & Boyd, 2017.*
Nine Titles – Ayr United triumphs, *Kennedy & Boyd, 2018.*
Ayr United; The Compendium, *Kennedy & Boyd, 2019.*

Ayr United -
The Oddest Matches

Duncan Carmichael

Kennedy & Boyd,
an imprint of
Zeticula Ltd,
Unit 13,
196 Rose Street,
Edinburgh,
EH2 4AT,
Scotland.

http://www.kennedyandboyd.co.uk
admin@kennedyandboyd.co.uk

First published in 2020
Copyright © Duncan Carmichael 2020
Cover design © Zeticula Ltd 2020

Photographs copyright © as credited

Every effort has been made to trace copyright holders of images. Any omissions will be corrected in future editions.

Paperback ISBN 978-1-84921-213-7

ACKNOWLEDGEMENTS

Illustrations are most useful for bringing a word picture to life and you will witness this principle being applied in the pages ahead. The history of Ayr United contains a vast amount of pictorial evidence and I consider myself lucky to possess so much of it.

Entire boxes of photos saved in digital form make for a good picture library but nonetheless some of the subject matter of this book required me to prevail on the kindness and co-operation of others.

David Sargent, you have my gratitude again. The slope at Beith really had to be seen to be believed. Your expert photography allows it to be seen...........and believed! I am further grateful for permitting the use of one of your photographs from a truly mad day at Forfar. In mentioning a mad day the theme of the book has been hinted at.

The first match featured in this book has Davy Russell as the central character. At Somerset Park in 1890 he was a veritable pantomime villain. His photograph is reproduced by kind permission of Paul Days. This particular image is proof that the player was not always coy about his identity.

DC Thomson is a wonderful organisation representing all that is wholesome in reading material. *The Sunday Post, Oor Wullie, The Broons, The Beano* – the list of reading pleasure could go on and on. I thank DC Thomson for allowing me to use a photograph from 1932. It shows the Ayr United players Fally Rodger and William McGrath. The image is beautifully nostalgic.

James Vance, I thank you for your kind permission to use your wonderful photo showing the volunteer builders at Somerset Park in 1950. It ties in nicely with the story about the wall disappearing in 2019.

The habitual thank you to the *Ayrshire Post* and the *Ayr Advertiser* will be repeated. Quotes and illustrations from both are punctuated throughout. Again these newspapers are to be thanked for their commendable Ayr United bias.

In 2020 Ayr United went through the club's longest non-playing period apart from the Second World War. Did we miss our visits to Somerset Park? Of course we did. It just goes to prove that life without Ayr United would be unthinkable. Failure to document the history would be equally unthinkable.

Duncan Carmichael
September 2020

CONTENTS

Illustrations

INTRODUCTION

Football has evolved on a massive scale. Transfer fees have reached the hundreds of millions and if the growth remains unchecked the sport will reach imponderable heights. The global pandemic of 2020 provided a stark illustration of the game's sense of priority. Mounting death rates failed to stifle the rapidly convened debates about the practicalities of getting football back up and running. Yet for all the game's burgeoning development and inflated sense of importance, we will never lose our love of those foibles and eccentricities which remind us of football's tendency to regress into its rawest format. The purpose of this book is to convey crazy goings-on in the history of Ayr United and, to a lesser degree, Ayr FC and Parkhouse. What happens when the goalkeeper doesn't turn up? What can be done when the ball bursts? Why did an opposition player don a disguise? The pages ahead are tantamount to a reality check. At any time football's pomposity is at threat of being ridiculed by happenings that bring it crashing right down to earth. That is when the talking point becomes the unspectacular rather than the spectacular. Football's unpredictability extends to far more than unexpected results. It has the capacity to create scenarios that could not even be dreamt of. Boxers versus Jockeys at Somerset Park – let that one sink in.

The circumstances of 2020 are thought to be unique yet there is a comparison with the winter of 1918/19 when a global epidemic of Spanish flu claimed more lives than the recently finished Great War. One of the victims was St. Mirren goalkeeper John Richardson who died at the age of twenty-four, precisely four weeks after playing in a match at Ayr. He died on the morning of an Airdrie versus St. Mirren fixture which went ahead as scheduled. This was after being stricken by the illness on the Wednesday. Back then the precautions bore no comparison with those imposed through Covid 19. The modern day precautions gave football a crazy look. This connects neatly to the premise of this book. It is about football with a crazy look. Moreover it is all true. You are about to read tales of the maddest matches.

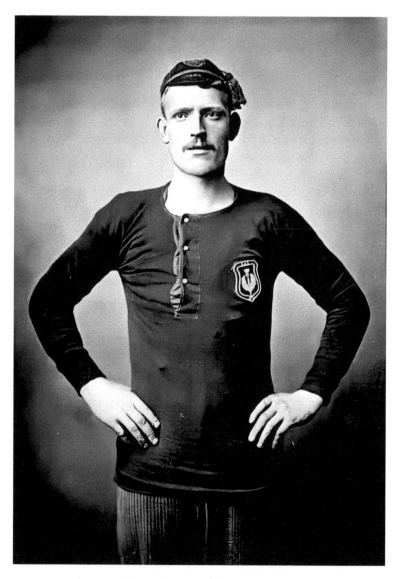

Davy Russell wearing his Scotland shirt in 1896 by which time he had no fear of recognition.

THE MASTER OF DISGUISE

Ayr FC versus Hearts – 8th November, 1890

You may be familiar with the novels of John Buchan. If so you will be aware of the great hero Richard Hannay whose skill in the art of disguise would frequently enable him to escape the clutches of hostile forces. It almost defies credibility that this is being mentioned in the context of an episode not drawn from fiction, especially since the scene of derring-do was Somerset Park.

On 16th August, 1890, the first batch of matches got played in the newly formed Scottish Football League. Less than three months later there was great excitement locally when it was learned that Hearts would be, in the words of the *Ayr Observer*, "The first of the clubs in the charmed league circle to visit the Auld Toon."

The event was a fourth round tie in the Scottish Cup. Three weeks earlier Ayr FC had defeated Clyde 4-3 at Barrowfield in the previous round. Much of the credit was heaped upon Fullarton Steele who had an effective but eccentric style of goalkeeping. The columns of the *Scottish Leader* contained this summary: "Perhaps the most noteworthy feature of the whole play was the unique goalkeeping of Steele for the winners. He is a perfect marvel and at times caused the greatest delight imaginable in clearing. Unlike other custodians Steele seldom uses his hands but he is a perfect wonder with his feet."

Hearts had the potential to provide sterner opposition than Clyde although both ties had factors in common. There was another 4-3 scoreline and Steele would again prove to be a major post match topic of conversation. The *Glasgow Herald* report made mention of the meteorological misery. "The weather was of the worst possible description for the game, rain falling through the whole of the game." Ross put the home team ahead with ten minutes played. By half-time the lead had been transformed into a deficit with Taylor (25) and Scott (35) scoring for Hearts. Begbie put his team 3-1 ahead then Ross scored for Ayr again. MacPherson made it 4-2 and again the two-goal deficit got trimmed when Hamilton scored. At 4-3 down the tie was alive with excitement. With ten minutes left that excitement peaked. Fullarton Steele saved a shot then threw the ball out. After the ball had left his hand a late challenge came from Davy Russell, the Hearts centre-forward. Russell collided with Steele who was left poleaxed on the ground. Some spectators behind that goal broke through the ropes. This was the cue for a break-in from all around the field. Russell was surrounded and assaulted but he managed to extricate himself from the mob then took flight. He took refuge in the Stand which backed onto the railway. (Somerset Park ran on a north-south alignment back then rather than the present day east-west alignment). Even this refuge was far from safe. The *Ayr Observer* report noted that a sympathiser in the Stand loaned him a hat and jacket. Thus disguised he cautiously found his way to the safety of the clubhouse. You may recall that ten minutes remained. The referee made a bold call in letting it restart since he too had been assaulted. Hearts had to play out the tie with ten men.

On 7th February, 1891, Hearts beat Dumbarton 1-0 in the Scottish Cup final, the venue being the second Hampden Park, later the site of Cathkin Park. The crowd was 10,836 and the scorer was the same Davy Russell. Were they worthy winners? Perhaps not. After their win at Ayr the *Ayr Observer* scribe concluded his report with the most candid of opinions: "Football as played by the Heart of Midlothian will soon bring the game into disgrace."

Fullarton Steele was unable to regale people with his adventures into old age. On 29th December, 1904, he passed away in Manchester. Ayr FC 3 Hearts 4. Scottish Cup 4th round.

Scorers: Ross 2, Hamilton.

THE GUARANTEED VICTORY

Parkhouse versus Dundee – 14th January, 1899

The heading implies that Parkhouse would definitely progress from this first round Scottish Cup tie against Dundee at Beresford Park. Why the certainty? The year of foundation for Dundee FC is 1893 yet when Parkhouse got drawn to play Dundee in 1899 it had already been reported that the Dundee club had met its demise. The popular view was that Parkhouse would therefore go through on a walkover. This was how the *Ayr Observer* summarised the scenario.

"It was generally conceded that Dundee, after their regrettable downfall, would scratch from the competition. There was a question of eligibility. Dundee as constituted after the collapse was not the club, in the true sense of the word, that had been nominated for the competition. Dundee decided to make the journey and in the event of victory on their side would test the legality of the point. Parkhouse protested before the game but, after winning, did not push the matter."

So there we have the key points. Dundee entered the Scottish Cup then the club folded. A newly constituted club adopted the name of Dundee Football Club and assumed the former club's place in the draw. Clearly that club was not eligible but they travelled to Ayr anyway, quite simply hoping for the best. Parkhouse would either win on the field or win via a protest. They could not lose. So let us see what happened next. This is how the *Daily Record* scribe reported it although he omitted detail of the final goal. He might have had a train to catch. If so he would not have had far to go. The description of the final goal has been borrowed from his *Glasgow Herald* counterpart.

"Once again an Ayrshire club has blighted the Dundee combination. It was Kilmarnock last year and now the amateurs of Ayr. The game was not by any means a brilliant one and with a change of venue Dundee, even with its mixed eleven, could easily have reversed matters. The only goal of the first half was unfortunately scored by Ferrier but it counted against the Tayside combination (own goal).

Dinsmore got a goal from a free-kick early in the second half and this practically won the match. Brown scored for Dundee (75th minute). Just on the call of time Spence scored for Parkhouse."

Note the reference to the mixed eleven. Their team had some players from the original Dundee club, one of whom was Sandy Keillor who played at left-half. He was formerly of Montrose and he had the rare distinction of appearing for Scotland while still with the Gable Endies.

After winning their 'could not lose' tie the second round draw brought Rangers to Beresford Park for a match that was highly likely to be lost. Rangers had already finished their league programme with a 100% record. It was a chilling thought that the visiting team would be close to full strength. The only regular missing was Neilly Gibson. Neilly was the father of Willie Gibson who would captain Ayr United to a Scottish Cup win over Rangers in 1923 then lift the FA Cup with Newcastle United the following year. The result was Parkhouse 1 Rangers 4 and compounding the misery was the half-time pass out check system being cancelled for the day. It was the custom for the fans to slip across to the Ayrshire and Galloway for a quick drink at half-time. It was definitely a quick drink since the half-time break lasted only ten minutes. When Rangers visited the scheme was rendered impractical by an attendance of 5,500. On this occasion there were no grounds for a protest against eligibility.

Parkhouse 3 Dundee 1. Scottish Cup 1st round.

Team: Brown, Dick, Orr, Mellon, Paton, Munachen, McCosh, Spence, Baird, Dinsmore and Boyd.

Scorers: Ferrier own goal, Harry Dinsmore, Billy Spence.

THE STAR GOALIE WHO DID NOT PLAY

Abercorn versus Ayr FC – 8th April, 1899

When season 1898/99 got underway there was no doubt that Hugh McDonald would retain his place in goal for Ayr FC. He was an outstanding goalkeeper who was destined to go on and play for Woolwich Arsenal. Port Glasgow Athletic won 3-2 at Ayr on Christmas Eve and McDonald lost his place. For the 1-0 win at home to Morton on Hogmanay the goalkeeper was Baxter who was described as "a Junior who hails from Dalry." Baxter retained a regular place until a 6-2 defeat away to Port Glasgow Athletic on 1st April, 1899. The goalkeeping curse associated with Port Glasgow struck again. For the fixture away to Abercorn one week later Baxter could not play due to an injury. A new goalkeeper by the name of Welsh was signed and he was listed to play against Abercorn.

John Byrne's history of Abercorn is a most informative read. He mentions that the club was founded on 10th November, 1877, and that their last match was played on 4th September, 1920. By then St. Mirren monopolised football interest in Paisley and Abercorn's appeal further suffered due to their all-too-convenient proximity to Ibrox. The visit of Ayr FC on 8th April, 1899, was historic. It was a Second Division fixture and it proved to be the last game at Underwood Park pending a move to Ralston Park. According to John Byrne: "The Cleansing Department needed the ground to erect a new destructor."

Let us resume the tale of Welsh's debut. It did occur but not until the following Saturday. He missed his train to Paisley. The Ayr team started with ten men in the hope that he would still arrive. Andy Davidson, normally a left-half, took up the position. The decision was then taken to send on McConnell to fill the outfield position vacated by Davidson. He had only just taken up his position on the field when Welsh appeared. With eleven men now on the field a switch was impossible. The timing was chronic. With the rhythm severely disturbed and playing against the wind it turned into a struggle. McLay, Robertson and Adam quickly put the home team 3-0 up. Connelly, Hyslop and Aitken scored in the second half to share the points in a 3-3 draw but there was an element of comedy which had not fully played out.

Although Welsh had not then appeared his name was on the team listings. National journalists took these listings for granted and they filed reports showing him as the goalkeeper. The journalists working for the *Ayrshire Post*, the *Ayr Advertiser* and the *Ayr Observer* knew fine well that the goalkeeper was Andy Davidson and their reports reflected this. On the Monday one of the national reports contained: "Welsh, Ayr's new goalkeeper, was in splendid form and was easily the best man on the field." It was an outstanding accolade for a player who would not make his debut until the following weekend. The committee resisted the temptation to let Davidson retain his place in goal.

Three weeks after the game at Underwood Park the teams met at Somerset Park in the Western League. The outcome was replicated. 3-0 for the home team at half-time and 3-3 at the end. An Abercorn scorer in that game at Ayr was John 'Sailor' Hunter, so-called because he had a rolling gait. Hunter was on the threshold of a fabulous career. Amongst his many accomplishments were scoring the winning goal for Dundee in the Scottish Cup final of 1910 and being the manager of Motherwell when they became league champions in 1932. In 1899 an accomplishment was scoring against Ayr goalkeeper Welsh but he failed to score against Andy Davidson, the man who was thought to have been Welsh!

Abercorn 3 Ayr FC 3. Scottish Second Division.

Team: Davidson, Wills, Doig, Millar, Ballantyne, McConnell, Dempsey, Aitken, Baird, Hyslop and Connelly.

Scorers: Connelly, Hyslop, Aitken.

THE CLUNE PARK QUITTERS

Port Glasgow Athletic versus Ayr FC – 6th January, 1900

Football pundits in the present day are apt to trot out the line that a particular ground is a difficult place to play. It is a clichéd line and it sometimes flies in the face of statistical analysis. However Clune Park in Port Glasgow genuinely was a formidable venue for opposition clubs. It sat at the foot of Clune Brae close by the Firth of Clyde. When Ayr FC arrived here for a Second Division fixture on the first Saturday of the twentieth century the chances of winning looked unfavourable. The club sat in seventh place out of ten with four wins, two draws and ten defeats. Port Glasgow Athletic were in a modest fifth position but historical precedent indicated that they would win this match. Since joining the Scottish League in 1897 Ayr FC had played at this ground on three occasions to date. The results were defeats of 4-1 (30th April, 1898), 6-2 (1st April, 1899) and 9-3 (13th May, 1899). That latter demise was in the Western League and the others were in the Second Division. Ayr FC had started shorthanded in the 9-3 game. Here in 1900 the home team would end shorthanded in scenes of extraordinary petulance.

By half-time the Clune Park bogey was laid to rest. By then it was 4-1, the scorers being Davidson, Munachen, Kelt and McAvoy. After taking the lead a goal was conceded when McCabe headed past Hugh McDonald from a Scullion corner-kick. Any encouragement the home team took from this was swiftly obliterated. The score in the second half replicated that in the first half. A Calder hat-trick and a goal from McAvoy took it to 8-2. When the eighth goal hit the net goalkeeper Ward did not bother retrieving it. He simply walked off the field in disgust. Outside-right Scullion took his place. Their number was now reduced to nine. Nine? Yes, nine! Right-half Martin had already walked off in a similar act of petulance. None of their players had been sent off and neither had any of them gone off through injury. The two of them simply decided that they had endured enough and retired themselves in a manner associated with cricket. If this were to happen today the story would go viral. Here in 1900 it paled in comparison to the column inches dedicated to the fierce battles taking place in the Boer War.

It could reasonably be assumed that the two errant players were then banished from Clune Park. This would be a wrong assumption. On the following Saturday Port Glasgow Athletic had a home tie against Falkirk in the first round of the Scottish Cup. They both played. Their 7-1 win prevented any further tantrums.

In the following season Ayr FC lost 5-0 in the league fixture at Port Glasgow. The next again season brought a 3-0 league defeat there. At the end of 1901/02 Port Glasgow Athletic got promoted as champions and Ayr FC had no further matches against that club.

After Ayr United got founded in 1910 the club's first competitive match was a Second Division fixture at home to the newly relegated Port Glasgow. It was a 2-0 win to Ayr United. Seven weeks later the clubs met at Clune Park and the result was a 1-0 defeat which came with the observation that: "The spectators maintained their reputation, both the referee and the Ayr United players coming in for some abuse from their tongues." No one alive will have any recollection of hostility at that ground. Under the weight of financial difficulties the club ceased in 1912.

Port Glasgow Athletic 2 Ayr FC 8. Second Division.

Team: McDonald, Wills, Johnstone, Munachen, Aitken, Davidson, Lindsay, Massey, Calder, McAvoy and Kelt.

Scorers: Davidson, Munachen, Kelt, McAvoy 2, Calder 3.

THE FOUR-POINT GAME

Ayr FC versus Motherwell – 8th December, 1900

Ayr FC had a fixture backlog caused by an over indulgence of cup football. In the Scottish Qualifying Cup Saturdays were used up in playing Hurlford (home), Annbank (away), Galston (away), Kilwinning Eglinton (home) Douglas Wanderers (home) and Stenhousemuir (home). That latter match proved to be the downfall when the tie was lost 2-1 at what was the semi-final stage. It was a defeat that had a refereeing controversy unforgotten for decades but that is another story. Also to this point of the season the first round of the Ayrshire Cup had occupied two Saturdays. The first leg had produced a 3-3 draw at home to Kilmarnock and the second leg was won 3-1 at Rugby Park. A draw would have wreaked yet more havoc on the schedules. When Motherwell came to Somerset Park on what was the second Saturday of December the Ayr club sat fourth in the Second Division having played merely six games comprising five wins and a defeat. The five wins had been at Ayr. (At the season's end the club found itself in the situation of having won every league game at home and losing every league game played away). The top three of St. Bernard's, Airdrie and Clyde had played twelve, thirteen and ten respectively by this stage. In the previous season the club had competed in the Scottish County League along with East Stirling, Raith Rovers, Hamilton Accies, Motherwell and Abercorn. When the season came to a close there remained one unplayed fixture in that league – Ayr FC versus Motherwell. It was decided that Motherwell's game at Somerset Park here in December would count towards the Scottish Second Division and the unplayed tie from 1899/00 in the Scottish County League. Four points were at stake even although two of them would apply to the season before.

The *Ayrshire Post* reported that: "Under auspices the very antithesis of favourable, the Ayr and Motherwell teams met at Somerset Park last Saturday." As if by way of translation this was qualified by: "Drenching rain was falling when the teams took the field." Motherwell played the first ten minutes without left-back McBride. His late arrival was inexcusable since he lived in Kilwinning. While playing a man short they employed a tactic known as the one-back system. This was an early day offside trap and it was successful for them at that point. Five minutes before half-time the home team took the lead with a header from a Lindsay corner-kick. Who scored? Who knows? After trawling through various reports you may be told that no one in the press seats knew. They could be excused. It was an overcast day, the rain continued to pour and there were no shirt numbers then. In the final minute of the first half Lindsay made it 2-0. The assembled press pack were unanimous on this. In the 68th minute Lindsay scored again and Reid netted for Motherwell shortly before the end. Four points were won in two competitions spread over two seasons.

Having a perfect home league record in a season when no away points were won was ample proof of the observation that: "The crossing of the Pow Burn has a singularly deteriorating effect on the form of the Ayr FC."

It was not the only time Motherwell lost four points on the one day. On 15th April, 1916, Ayr United won 3-0 in what was the club's first ever league win at Fir Park. Having played Ayr United in the afternoon they then had to play Celtic in the evening, again in the league and also at Fir Park. In the afternoon Celtic had beaten Raith Rovers 6-0 in a league fixture at Celtic Park. It being the second game for both clubs it all seemed fair. Celtic won 3-1. Having lost four points on the one day in 1900 they lost four points on the one day in 1916.

Ayr FC 3 Motherwell 1. Second Division/Scottish County League.

Team: Hugh McDonald, John McDonald, Wills, Stevenson, Aitken, Allan, Tom Kennedy, Massey, Sam Kennedy, McAvoy and Lindsay.

Scorers: -----, Lindsay 2.

THE BLOCKS

Hurlford versus Ayr FC – 6th September, 1902

When Ayr FC got drawn to play at Hurlford in the first round of the Scottish Qualifying Cup there was doubt as to whether the tie would even take place. When the 1902/03 season got underway Hurlford had no ground. At the same stage of the competition two years earlier Hurlford had to relinquish home advantage and play Ayr FC at Somerset Park. They did have a ground then but it was not enclosed. In 1902 the doubt over viability was allayed when the tie was arranged for Wellington Park in Crookedholm, the home of Hurlford Thistle. This ground was nicknamed The Blocks. The Ayr squad arrived at Kilmarnock Station then made the onward journey by horse-drawn brakes and waggonettes. It is unlikely that defeat would have been considered since the team was fresh from a 5-0 rout of Raith Rovers in a Second Division fixture at Somerset Park. The Ayr support viewed the tie apathetically. It was estimated that only about fifty bothered to travel. Even at league level some of the visiting grounds were in a poor state but Wellington Park was downright shocking. On arrival it was necessary to negotiate a steep slope down to the field. In fact the *Ayrshire Post* reporter described his descent as "an athletic feat." The playing surface was not roped off down one side and along one end. Playing surface? Well that was what they called it. It was an undulating field of coarse grass. The pitch markings were a complete mess. For example the lines for the goal areas were drawn from the goalposts rather than six yards to the side of them. The *Ayr Observer* reporter was even more scathing than his *Ayrshire Post* counterpart: "There was some dubiety for a time as to Hurlford's being able to toe the mark owing to ground difficulties, but ultimately getting possession of a nondescript enclosure termed in irony a park, Ayr had perforce to travel. If he is to be believed, the average Ayr supporter present would scorn having such a piece of waste ground at his back door. A long delay was caused by the referee rejecting the ball which was to duty during the afternoon and its having to be repaired. Ayr protested before the start against the eccentricities of the line markings."

The protest of course would only be proceeded with in the event of defeat. This gave the potential for a situation in which they could not lose. Defeat could certainly have been excused since they were playing with a patched-up ball on a lumpy field of rough grass. About 250 people paid to watch the tie but a number higher than that watched for free and it was ironic that the non-paying spectators had a better view. The entrance to the field was also the entrance to a right of way that ran alongside the railway. People were therefore entitled to pass into the ground whether they were there to watch the football or not. Only those who clambered down the hill were charged.

Jimmy Hay scored in the third minute. The state of the pitch could hardly have been worse than the condition of Pebble Park in his days playing for Annbank. Before the season was finished he was destined for loftier things with a transfer to Celtic where he would captain that club to six consecutive league titles. He was also destined to captain Newcastle United and Scotland. A second goal came ten minutes later. Stevenson, the scorer, would have been known to some of the home supporters. He lived in Hurlford. James Gillespie scored in the 32nd minute at which point a rout may have been anticipated. The result was a modest 3-1. This had to be considered satisfactory on a pitch that railed against flowing football. The reason why Wellington Park was nicknamed The Blocks is open to your own interpretation, although it might not be too difficult to discern.

Hurlford 1 Ayr FC 3. Scottish Qualifying Cup 1st round.

Team: Hugh McDonald, John McDonald, Wills, Stevenson, Aitken, Miller, Gillespie, Drain, Hay, White and Young.

Scorers: Jimmy Hay, Stevenson, James Gillespie.

THE EPIC JOURNEY

Albion Rovers versus Ayr FC – 21st November, 1903

How can Albion Rovers away be an epic journey? Please read on.

In season 1903/04 Ayr FC had a successful if sometimes tortuous run in the Scottish Qualifying Cup.

In the first round bitter local rivals Parkhouse were beaten 1-0 at Somerset Park after a 0-0 draw at Beresford Park.

The bye in the second round was solely on account of there being an uneven number of teams in the draw.

In the third round there was a fortuitous 1-1 draw at home to Galston. Hugh Kerr's equaliser came so late that a lot of supporters had already left the ground therefore a story circulated that it was a 1-0 defeat. The saving goal left the Ayr crowd "frantic with joy." Scorer Kerr was in his first season with the club after signing from Westerlea but he would not see the season out.

On 6th January, 1904, he was transferred to the club formerly known as Newton Heath but by then they were in their second season as Manchester United. On 10th April, 1918, he died from wounds suffered at the Western Front.

Back in 1903 the replayed tie at Galston's Riverside Park was scoreless. The second replay was won 2-0 at Somerset Park. Three consecutive Saturdays playing Galston was evidence indeed that it was tortuous. The next two Saturdays also involved Scottish Qualifying Cup business. Kilwinning Eglinton (2-1) and Nithsdale Wanderers (3-0) were conquered at Ayr in rounds four and five respectively.

The semi-final draw contained a quartet of 'A's; Ayr FC, Albion Rovers, Arbroath and Albion Rovers. It was a kind draw, Albion Rovers at home. Of the estimated 6,000 crowd there was an away support of about 1,500. They had two chartered trains. It was 0-0 so the action reverted to Meadow Park the following Saturday. The ground name was a misnomer. The Albion Rovers ground had a pitch reminiscent of a gluepot.

Ayr FC 14th November, 1903, the date of the original tie against Albion Rovers.

Rear left to right: Un-named reserve, Hugh McDonald, Drain, Young, John McDonald, Glendinning (committee), Wills, William McDonald, Moffat, Cunningham (trainer), Alexander (committee) and Taylor (secretary).

Seated left to right: Gillespie, McCurdie, Aitken, Stevenson, Hay and Mathie.

The trophy is the Ayr Charity Cup. When Ayr FC won it in the year of its inception (1885) the goalkeeper was Joseph Glendinning who is seen here as a committee man and a winger in that team was Bobby Cunningham who is the trainer shown.

It being the third Saturday in November, the advertised kick-off time was 2.30pm. The special train for the Ayr support was scheduled to leave Ayr Station at 12.15pm. It pulled out half an hour late. Frustrating though it was, there should still have been enough time to get to Coatbridge and imbibe in a local pub before the match, as was the custom of the average supporter in the Edwardian era. However, as the journey progressed, thoughts turned merely to getting to the game on time. The word 'progressed' is ill-chosen on this page. In his description of the journey the *Ayr Observer* reporter showed his mastery of Scotland's capacity for sarcasm.

"There was little delay at Ayr Station but the journey was painfully slow. One could have golfed along the links at the railway side so to speak. A fairly large number of supporters joined the train at Newton on Ayr but the Prestwick and Troon crowd would not have made a couple of tug of war teams. The wind must have been very strong to impede the progress of the train."

Meadow Park was in the Whifflet area of Coatbridge. Ayr United supporters of today will know Whifflet as the first part of Coatbridge they come to when approaching from the direction of East Kilbride. The chartered train pulled into Whifflet Station at 3.30pm. This was one hour after the game had started and two and three-quarter hours after it had left Ayr. Our *Ayr Observer* informant tells us: "Not one of the Ayr folks would see more than thirty minutes of the game and most saw less." The exodus towards the ground was akin to the survival of the fittest. Those possessed of some athleticism left the less mobile struggling behind.

A bad day was about to get worse. The home team opened the scoring twenty minutes from the end, much of the Ayr support having barely arrived in the ground. It was a goal greatly appreciated by the bulk of the 7,000 crowd. There was no comeback. It ended 1-0. The other semi-final was also decided that day, Arbroath beating Alloa Athletic 4-0 at Gayfield. In the final Arbroath beat Albion Rovers 4-2 at Dundee.

Three days after losing at Coatbridge, Ayr FC captain Tom Wills signed for Newcastle United. In the summer of 1906 he was transferred to Crystal Palace. During season 1906/07 he moved to Carlisle United and at the end of that campaign he went full circle by rejoining Ayr FC. 21st November, 1903, was inglorious in his playing career but it was even more inglorious for the fans who were driven to breaking point. His full-back partner was Alex Moffat whose last playing season at first team level was 1905/06. He went on to have a massively long connection to Somerset Park. In 1923 he joined the Ayr United board and remained until opting not to seek re-election at the annual general meeting on 27th July, 1965. A boyhood memory is of supporters talking about "old Mr Moffat".

Albion Rovers 1 Ayr FC 0. Scottish Qualifying Cup semi-final.

Team: Mathie, Moffat, Wills, Stevenson, McDowall, Watson, Walls, Irvine, Kerr, White and Hamilton

A PARAGON OF VIRTUE

Leith Athletic versus Parkhouse – 22nd August, 1908

It is well known that Ayr United's nickname is the Honest Men. Ayr FC and Parkhouse, the two clubs in the merger, both carried the same nickname. Sometimes Ayr FC would be called the Auldtonians and there were references to Parkhouse being called the Parkies. Clubs did not choose nicknames. They were coined by the press to prevent staidness in match reports. Yet for Parkhouse the Honest Men label could not have been more apt. Their Beresford Park location was in the more genteel part of the town, south of the river. Similarly their support was drawn from the more prosperous districts. Rightly or wrongly gentlemen have a reputation for fair play. What happened in this game left the Parkhouse club with a reputation for being morally spotless.

It was Parkhouse's opening engagement in the Second Division campaign of 1908/09 and the venue was Logie Green which was not in Leith but a bit to the west of that area. The league had got underway on the previous Saturday, Leith winning 3-1 away to East Stirling. Parkhouse missed the opening day on account of having to play at home to Galston in an Ayrshire Cup semi-final deferred from 1907/08. The ignominy of losing 2-1 was compounded by having to kick-off at 6.15pm due to the counter attraction of a race meeting.

In the Leith match there was a stoppage when Charlie Phillips got injured after a tackle by home centre-half Winning. Phillips was a small player with a lean build but he was agile and clever. Too clever for the Leith stopper! Closer inspection of the injury indicated that his leg had been gashed by the boot of his adversary. Winning was sent off. At least the referee tried to send him off. The defiant perpetrator stood his ground. Immediately there was an altercation. Given the physical nature of Scottish football in Edwardian times sendings-off were rare in comparison to the game in the 21st century. It really did take something particularly violent to get sent from the field. The *Ayr Observer* report went so far as to accuse the referee of "causing a sensation" by pointing the player in the direction of the pavilion. It really did look as if he had no intention of leaving the field anyway. The president of Leith Athletic then walked onto the field, not to remonstrate with his player but to remonstrate with the referee. A discussion ensued whilst an onfield demonstration continued. During all the carry-on the errant player decided to leave the field of his own accord.

While playing with ten men Leith scored. The marksman was inside-right Ritchie. This story would have had a more exotic touch if the scorer had been his team mate at centre-forward, the wonderfully named Colombo. Every player in the home team possessed a typically Scottish surname except the striker. As proof here is the listing: Kinghorn, Brown, Paterson, Kane, Winning, Moffat, Lindsay, Ritchie, Colombo, Dewar and O'Brien. Leith Athletic in 1908 and we have such an exotic name.

When the teams came out for the second half it was noticed that Leith had eleven players. Why had a sent-off player reappeared? This may seem beyond belief but he was back on at the instigation of the Parkhouse committee. In a normal world the visiting delegation would have been preoccupied by the 1-0 deficit and what could be done by way of getting back into the game. The Parkhouse committee did not live in a normal world. Their half-time task involved consulting with the Leith committee and telling them that they would share the responsibility for Winning's reappearance because they considered the sending-off too drastic. You, the reader, have read that correctly. The Parkhouse representatives were vigorously campaigning to make a hard match even harder for themselves. These developments were conveyed to the referee and he offered no opposition to the player going back on.

It is difficult to comprehend why anyone, far less the opposition, would have been adamant that the dismissal was an injustice. The gash on Charlie Phillips' leg was caused by a combination of a bad challenge and illegal footwear. Winning was playing with a nail protruding through a stud. The *Ayr Observer* scribe was knowledgeable enough to cite a rule that players with defective footwear should be kept off. No further scoring took place so Parkhouse returned home with a 1-0 loss but with honour intact.

In the same season Parkhouse lost 9-0 to Dundee at Dens Park in a first round Scottish Cup tie. Once again we are indebted to the man from the *Ayr Observer* for an insight: "Parkhouse played a clean game without any semblance of roughness." Even an annihilation could not disturb their reputation for sporting integrity. Sporting integrity! This is a much hyped phrase in the present day and we can only wonder why. Players will hit the ground when there has been little or no contact. A posse of players will turn mob handed on a referee. We even see players kick the ball over the touchline then have the effrontery to claim the throw. Such histrionics were lost on the olden-day Parkhouse. Their halo shone ever bright.

Leith Athletic 1 Parkhouse 0. Second Division.

Team: A. Black, Lean, W. Black, Burns, Tickle, Potter, Lynch, Phillips, Stevenson, McLean and Goodwin.

Lee Massey – Ayr United's first goalkeeper.

THE DIY GROUND

Dumfries versus Ayr United – 2ⁿᵈ September, 1911

Dumfries FC was one of the three clubs involved in the amalgamation to form Queen of the South in 1919. In the years of their existence their Eastfield ground had the advantage of being conveniently located in close proximity to the railway station. Advantage number two? There was no advantage number two. Or if there was it was unapparent in 1911. The ground was far from bowling-green quality. It was "small and lumpy" according to a contemporary report. This was the second season of Ayr United's existence but the club's Second Division status did not permit exemption from the Scottish Qualifying Cup. One year to the weekend earlier (3ʳᵈ September, 1910) the clubs had met in the first round of that competition in what was Ayr United's first cup match at Somerset Park and our second ever competitive match at the sacred ground. On that occasion Sam Graham and Charlie Howe had scored in a 2-0 win. The fact that the clubs were drawn together at the same stage in 1911 was open to ambiguity. Yes it was the same round but the actual stage was an apology for a football field. The seating accommodation was described as "a midget stand" and the same report mentioned that it was "soon crushed full." Officials of the home club then employed desperate efforts to provide more seating. With dubious ingenuity seats were fashioned out of planks, railway sleepers, club baskets, pails and boxes. The Taylor Report carried extensive recommendations for seating at football grounds when published in 1990. We can be absolutely certain that this was not the type of seating Lord Justice Taylor had in mind.

A special train ran from Ayr for this match and the journey through the valley of the Nith made a huge impression on the large number who had never travelled that way before. After the passengers had been disgorged at Dumfries the impression was somewhat more subdued after the short walk to the ground. Even by the standards of 1911 it was a poor spectacle. Harry Simpson scored six minutes before half-time yet it ended 1-1. With home advantage for the following

Saturday there was a mood of optimism for the replay. The optimism was justified. On the more even contours of Somerset Park a 5-1 win was achieved in which Charlie Phillips scored four. Hugh Logan also scored. The eccentricities of round one carried over into round two. Whithorn got beaten 10-0 at Ayr in a tie so one-sided that goalkeeper Massey and full-backs McKenzie and Gardner took it in turn to pose for a photographer while the game was actually in progress. Please remember that photographic processes in 1911 were cumbersome. There was a lot more too it then a quick wave to the camera. Any eccentricities in round three? Yes! Thornhill were beaten 7-2 and the visitors brought a real goat to Somerset Park as a mascot.

Dumfries 1 Ayr United 1. Scottish Qualifying Cup 1st round.

Team: Massey, McKenzie, Gardiner, Connell, Tickle, McLaughlan, Goodwin, Logan, Phillips, Simpson and Campbell.

Scorer: Harry Simpson.

Hugh Logan scoring in the replay on 9th September, 1911.

WHERE IS OUR KIT? DUNDEE!

Aberdeen versus Ayr United – 25ᵗʰ October, 1913

Having the kit in Dundee is fine when the team is actually playing in Dundee. When the team is playing in Aberdeen it is the stuff of nightmares. The Ayr United players and directors arrived at Pittodrie high in confidence. In the previous match Motherwell had been thrashed 4-0 at Somerset Park. Aberdeen were foundering in second bottom place in the First Division with just one league victory to this point of the season.

It was the club's first visit to this ground, albeit that predecessors Ayr FC had played in this location. In fact Ayr FC had played a major role in Aberdeen becoming a league club in the first place. At the end of season 1903/04 Parkhouse had to apply for re-election to the Second Division. The secretary of Ayr FC sent a circular to the voting clubs outlining why they considered that no support should be accorded to their fellow townsmen. Parkhouse did lose their league place and the vacancy was filled by Aberdeen. When the story of the plot was revealed the hatred between the Ayr clubs sunk to even more unfathomable depths.

In 1913 the area of land adjoining Pittodrie may have reminded the Ayr party of home. It was next to the beach and it had a striking similarity to Ayr's Low Green. Yet they were not here as tourists. The more serious matter of First Division duty awaited but there was one pressing issue to be addressed. Where was the kit? Telephone enquiry solicited the information that it had been offloaded at Dundee. With kick-off time closing in and the hamper seventy miles away it was surely just a matter of borrowing spare kit from the home club. Aberdeen FC duly obliged with a set of white shirts and white shorts. The home team's colours were then black and gold striped shirts and white shorts thereby making it a striking contrast.

What about the boots? This was the Pittodrie of 1913. There was not a hope of spare boots. A delegation of Ayr United directors frantically made haste to a shop in Union Street. There was little deliberation over their purchase. Eleven pairs of football boots please! In the earnest hope that the correct sizes had been purchased the haul was soon deposited in the away dressing room. Let us take stock. White shirts, white shorts and new boots – what about the socks? Thankfully this was in an age when ankle socks were not in fashion therefore the hosiery worn was simply what the players had travelled in.

Willie McStay sporting the mislaid kit.

In the early stages of the game the Ayr United team looked emboldened while Aberdeen struggled to cope with the superior pace. The team's normal garb was a less invigorating hotchpotch comprising shirts of crimson and gold hoops and blue shorts. Charlie Phillips was a centre-forward who had played for West Ham United. Critical reporters were apt to mention his lack of physique but this was no handicap to him, even in the harsh world of olden-day football. He beat goalkeeper Andy Greig with a header to establish the lead. Within five minutes of half-time Aberdeen equalised through Angus McLeod then took the lead with a Jock Wyllie goal. Charlie Phillips scored again in the second half then the team had to hold on for a hard fought draw. The kit drama and consequent late kick-off caused the game to finish in semi-darkness. Ayr United's borrowed kit still managed to be visible in the descending gloom.

Unfortunately the club eventually got reunited with the drab kit. This was, however, the last season in which the old Ayr FC shirts and the old Parkhouse shorts were worn. In August 1914 the board announced the new club colours of black and white.

Aberdeen 2 Ayr United 2. First Division.

Team: Woods, Bell, McStay, McDougall, Bannister, McLaughlan, Middleton, Robertson, Phillips, McGowan and Gray.

Scorer: Charlie Phillips 2.

THE PUB RUN

Ayr United versus Hibs – 28ᵗʰ August, 1915

During the Great War pub opening hours were severely restricted. One of the more obvious reasons was the danger of people working in munitions factories when they were the worse for wear. However contemporary reports also tell of a view that some of the ingredients of beer were more appropriate to food production, principally barley, hops and yeast. The practice of treating was made illegal. This was the olden-day expression for buying a round. Ayr United opened season 1915/16 with a 2-0 defeat away to Dundee. The following Saturday's visit from Hibs then caused chaos owing to the issue of pub opening hours.

A Government initiative meant that pubs had to synchronise their opening times with the kick-off time at local football matches. This rendered pre-match drinks impossible. By law the pubs in Ayr could only open their doors at the exact time of the kick-off at Somerset Park. In polite society this would not create a problem but to the Ayr United fans of 1915 it was a major problem. The logical solution would have been to go to the game then go to the pub. For a large swathe of fans this was out of the question. The custom was to go to the pub then head for the game. Anything else would not be considered. So here is what happened.

When the game kicked-off the crowd inside Somerset Park looked as if it did not even top 2,000. Reinforcements were on the way. Lots of them! Queues of men were seen outside pub doors before they were opened. The scene was the same at the various nearby hostelries. When the doors were opened a stampede to the bar ensued. You will recall from the opening paragraph that each drink had to be bought individually but prudent publicans already had lines of drinks poured. For proximity to the ground the sensible option would have been the Olympia Bar situated right at the junction of George Street and King Street. Drinking is a leisure pursuit but there was nothing leisurely about the pace these drinks were consumed at. The next development was hordes of men spilling out of the various pubs and racing to Somerset Park having sacrificed the early part of the match for a very swift drink.

Something similar happened on 1st March, 1967. This was a Wednesday and a First Division match at home to Motherwell kicked-off at four o'clock which coincided with the time that the schools finished. The bell at Ayr Academy had barely stopped ringing when there was a frantic exodus through the school gates. Your writer had no particular aptitude for running but right then sufficient reserves of energy were employed in the scramble to Somerset Park. After crossing the New Bridge an Annbank bus was spotted turning into River Street. It was impeccably timed and heading in the direction of Whitletts Road. On breathlessly entering the ground the news was that it was 1-1. It finished 3-3.

Retracing our steps back to 1915 the question must be asked. Were the drinkers rewarded for their efforts? The answer is no. Jimmy Richardson scored twice but Hibs won 3-2. These were harrowing times. At Dundee the week before the Ayr United party arrived at the station just in time to witness a Red Cross train on an adjacent platform. Ninety wounded men had been brought from Southampton and they were taken to the infirmary in a series of ambulance waggons.

A fortnight before the season had started an *Ayrshire Post* editorial contained some forthright comment.

"It is not a case of business as usual. The carrying on of the game at all, with the European war raging fiercely, has brought condemnatory protests in many quarters. It may happen that the course of the war will render necessary a stoppage of football, but it is to be hoped that Great Britain and her allies will soon succeed in choking off the German Huns and those associated with them."

Ayr United 2 Hibs 3. First Division.

Team: Kerr, Bell, Semple, Nevin, Getgood, McLaughlan, Ingram, Crosbie, Richardson, McBain and Gray.

Scorer: Jimmy Richardson 2.

IT'S YOUR TURN TO GO IN GOAL

Ayr United versus Celtic – 2nd September, 1916

One week earlier Ayr United had started with ten men at Firhill. Outside-left Alec Gray eventually appeared on the pitch with twenty-four minutes played and Partick Thistle 1-0 ahead. The damage did not end there. It was the occasion of a 3-0 defeat.

Ayr United versus Celtic on 2nd September, 1916.

For the visit of Celtic the threat of starting with ten men in consecutive games reared itself with the non-appearance of goalkeeper Gordon Kerr. Since April he had been Private Kerr of the appropriately named Gordon Highlanders. He was stationed in Aberdeen but had remained as a regular in the Ayr United goal through an extraordinary leniency in allowing him leave to take part in games.

Travelling though could prove awkward in war time. Trains carrying troops or munitions always gained precedence over passenger transport so the possibility of delays always existed. The fact that Ayr United took the field with ten men indicated a hope that Kerr would appear. Quite charitably the referee allowed the game to start fifteen minutes late. John Bell, normally a right-back, took up the goalkeeping position. Joe O'Kane scored for Celtic in the third minute. He benefited from the space created by Bell's absence from his conventional position. Soon after the goal Billy Middleton appeared on the field. This increased the complement to eleven but Middleton was a forward. Bell's absence at full-back was clearly more crucial than Middleton's absence as a forward. The latter took over in goal and remained there until the end. Moreover he kept a clean goal and even the Old Firm-centric Glasgow press admitted that Ayr United were unlucky to lose 1-0. For example the *Glasgow Herald* referred to "the Celts' rather fortunate escape at Ayr."

Of course being 1916 there were more potent woes at large. As a reminder this game was witnessed by wounded soldiers who were accommodated with seats at the front of the Stand. This links neatly to future events on the Western Front that would prevent any possibility of Billy Middleton dabbling in goalkeeping again. On 9th May, 1917, a letter was received stating that he had a wounded left arm and that he was in a makeshift hospital in France. This handicap had not prevented him from writing the letter to Ayr United himself. Although a native of West Boldon, County Durham, he was serving with the Ayrshire Yeomanry. He was patched up and returned to the trenches. In April 1918 word was received that his left hand was so badly shot that his war was over. On his return to the Ayr United team his old form was recaptured and in 1920 he was transferred to Aberdeen but the damage to his left arm and left hand guaranteed that he would never again be pressed into emergency goalkeeping duties.

Readers may have had experience of turning up to play football for a team with no goalkeeper. This is more likely to happen in the indoor game. The procedure for this occurrence normally involves players taking it in turn to play in goal until they concede then someone else takes over. Let us recap. Against Celtic in 1916 John Bell was the unwilling goalkeeper until conceding early in the match. Billy Middleton took over and he did not concede at all.

This is not to suggest that he would otherwise have been relieved of his goalkeeping duties but we can safely attribute this episode to the vagaries of wartime. Anyway it is now time for a happy ending. The following Saturday the result was Kilmarnock 1 Ayr United 2. Middleton revelled in the restoration of his outfield freedom by scoring twice.

Ayr United 0 Celtic 1. First Division.

Team: Middleton, Bell, Hay, Waddell, Willie Cringan, McLaughlan, Ingram, Crosbie, Marshall, Robert Cringan and Gray.

THE DELIBERATE OWN GOAL

Airdrie versus Ayr United – 22ⁿᵈ December, 1917

The heading has an inconsistent look. How can an own goal be deliberate? These are surely just unlucky mishaps or errors of judgement. However this is the tale of a player who deliberately scored against his own team.

Season 1917/18 was wretched for most clubs. The more pressing issue of the war made for player shortages and less fans coming into the ground. For Ayr United it was a season more wretched than most other clubs. The completed First Division table showed the club with the wooden spoon. At the end of season annual general meeting William Ferguson, the chairman, bemoaned the difficulties attendant on carrying on. He mentioned too that only once had it been possible to turn out the same team on two consecutive Saturdays. This was a build-up to his admission that the financial loss had been considerable.

Peace on earth is the usual festive refrain. At Christmas time in 1917 that notion was a joke and not a very funny one. Goodwill to all men – let us leave that one right there! Christmas Day landed on a Tuesday that year. On the Saturday prior to it Ayr United turned up to play Airdrie in a league fixture at Broomfield Park. The depression surrounding the season so far was a microcosm of the national mood. In the various theatres of war the fighting was grim and the casualty lists were beyond horrendous. It may have been a hugely lesser priority but the team arrived at Airdrie having scored only one goal from the last seven games. Jimmy Richardson remains Ayr United's third highest scorer of league goals despite missing more than two seasons due to active service. At this time he was Corporal James Richardson and he was at the Western Front. The team's goal drought in 1917/18 would not have occurred had he not been away doing his bit for King and country. Football during the war was filled with such vagaries and in mentioning this it is appropriate to acknowledge the importance of priority.

Jimmy Richardson

By the time of this match at Airdrie no Ayr United centre-forward had registered a goal all season (excepting a charity match against a Junior Select in August). Please be reminded of the date. 22nd December! Steele, a first season senior signed from Glenburn Rovers, failed in the first four matches. For league fixture five Jimmy Richardson played in a one-off match while home on leave but, rarely for him, he did not score in the 1-1 draw away to Third Lanark, one of his former clubs. Thereafter the centre-forwards who failed to hit the target in successive league games were McNaughton, Steele again and Webb. Webb had a poor debut away to St. Mirren but the scarcity of resources was so bad that he got retained for a home match with Falkirk. That match was won 4-0 but the curse of the centre-forwards was still not broken. Steele again, Bennett, Hardie, Bennett again, Somerville, then Gibbon for four consecutive matches – still the succession of Ayr United centre-forwards could not score. Bennett was the famous Alex Bennett who had played for Celtic, Rangers and Scotland.

The situation was so desperate that for the fixture at Airdrie a centre-forward had to be borrowed from the home club. He scored, albeit that Ayr United lost 4-1. The first centre-forward to score for Ayr United all season was a player called Neilson who netted against his own club. This should make sense of the heading. He deliberately scored against his own team! Three games later, on 5th January, 1918, there was a 3-0 away win against Hamilton Accies and Billy Middleton, playing at centre-forward, scored twice. At last we had a goal from a centre-forward of our own.

Airdrie 4 Ayr United 1. First Division.

Team: Lock, Semple, Brock, Crosbie, Somerville, McLaughlan, Morton, Devine, Neilson, Bennett and Middleton.

Scorer: Neilson.

A cartoonist with a warning of caution on the eve of the Rangers tie.

THE DAY THE BALL BURST

Ayr United versus Rangers – 27ᵗʰ January, 1923

It will have been the boyhood experience of many of us. A 'jackets for goalposts' game in the park suffers a lamentable halt because the ball has burst. It may have been a cheap ball in the first place or it may have been a once-decent ball patched up too many times. Another scenario was the stray dog sinking its teeth into it. Such were the vagaries of impromptu games in the park. Half-time came when a team scored five. Full time was when a team scored ten or when teatime came, whichever was the soonest.

On 29ᵗʰ August, 1993, your writer interviewed John McCosh who was then aged eighty-nine. He had been at the Ayr United versus Dumbarton match on the previous day but it is more pertinent to relate that he was a centre-forward who had played for Coylton Juveniles and Auchinleck Talbot before signing for Ayr United. His first team debut was away to Dumbarton on 26ᵗʰ September, 1925. He said that when he was a boy in his native Coylton (he pronounced it in the Ayrshire vernacular as 'Culton') he used to play football in his bare feet with a ball comprising an inflated pig's bladder obtained from Ayr Slaughterhouse. It was held together by thread.

The concept of a burst ball in senior football is rare. With the potential for reputational damage to the manufacturer the ball just has to be of the highest quality. This much is reflected in the price. Even back in 1923 it would not have crossed a spectator's mind that the ball would burst at a professional game. Yet in that year it happened at Somerset Park in what was a massive game.

When Rangers visited for a third round Scottish Cup tie the crowd of 15,853 set a new record for the ground. That figure would have been even higher had it not been for people staying away for fear that they would not get in. It remained a record only until the following year. On 9ᵗʰ February, 1924, 16,721 turned up for a Scottish Cup win over Kilmarnock. The Rangers game was huge. Their Golden Jubilee was celebrated in 1923 and their centenary was celebrated

Tommy Kilpatrick.

in 1973. Quite why their year of foundation was later revised from 1873 to 1872 is a question for their club historians. The relevance here is that they were hoping to win a league and cup double to coincide with their Golden Jubilee (or what they thought their Golden Jubilee was!). This did not happen because they were drawn to play at Ayr in the cup. Ayr United refused a financial inducement to switch the tie to Ibrox. This type of bribe was actually quite legal in 1923.

On a dull but dry day Ayr United took to the field first. Willie Gibson, the captain, was at the head of the column. On winning the toss Gibson opted for wind advantage in the first half. The tie then kicked-off in an atmosphere of great anticipation. This excitement quickly became an anti-climax. The action had been underway for no more than several minutes when the ball burst on the spikes of the barricade at the edge of the pitch. A 1923-style football was sturdy. To convey just how sturdy we can refer to the worn old cliché that it was like a medicine ball on a wet day. Admittedly this was not a wet day but the ground had been rendered heavy by earlier rain. In the contest between a metal spike and heavy leather there was only going to be one winner. The burst ball was testament to this. What an embarrassment! This was not a spontaneously arranged kickabout in Northfield Park. It was a high profile Scottish Cup tie. A replacement was found and it met the approval of referee William Bell.

Murdoch McKenzie (71) and John McLean (73) put Ayr United on course for a 2-0 win. Ten of the team had been signed from Junior clubs. The exception was Tommy Kilpatrick who was formerly of Hibs and Dundee. A fortnight later a 2-0 defeat away to Third Lanark attracted a crowd of 36,000. It was Scotland's biggest crowd that afternoon. Captain Willie Gibson therefore failed to get his hands on the Scottish Cup in 1923 but he was in Newcastle United's FA Cup winning team of 1924 as well as being a regular when they won the Football League in 1926/27.

The win over Rangers ensured that the burst ball was forgotten – until now! In January 1973 your writer had the privilege of interviewing a veteran of that team. The player was James McLean who, at the time, lived in the Muirhead district of Troon.

Ayr United 2 Rangers 0. Scottish Cup 2nd round.

Team: Nisbet, Smith, McCloy, Hogg, McLeod, Gibson, Kilpatrick, Cunningham, John McLean, McKenzie and James McLean.

Scorers: Murdoch McKenzie, John McLean.

Willie Gibson.

A different cartoonist at work
after the 1923 cup win

THE ULTIMATE MISMATCH

Boxers versus Jockeys – 15th July, 1929

At this time the Railway End enclosure was four years away from being opened but in 1929 fund raising events were already underway. On this particular Monday evening there was a sports meeting at Somerset Park. It was arranged by the Ayr United Supporters' Club and the object was to get money into the coffers for the proposed enclosure. The date could not have been better chosen. 15th July was the hottest day of the year so far and it was Glasgow Fair Monday. Trains heading out of Glasgow were packed. Convoys of buses left the city too. Ayr faced competition from such resorts as Helensburgh, Largs, Saltcoats, Dunoon and Rothesay but the town managed to get an ample share of excursionists. The town was besieged. Sports meetings were highly popular and with so many tourists in circulation the guarantee of a good attendance at Somerset Park materialised.

The highlight of the evening was a novelty event. It was a Boxers versus Jockeys football match. Just contemplate that for a moment. Think of the difference in physique. The referee was the illustrious Dixie Dean. He remains the only player to have scored sixty goals in a Football League season. That was in 1927/28, the same season in which Jimmy Smith scored sixty-six goals for Ayr United in the Scottish Second Division. For this novelty match Dixie Dean had Jimmy Smith as a linesman. The other linesman was Tommy McInally who made his name with Celtic but who had more recently been playing for Sunderland. McInally had played on loan for Ayr United in 1917.

A boxer by the name of McMillan scored all six in his team's 6-5 win. One of the jockeys who scored was Harry Wragg whose name was to become synonymous with Partick Thistle through the advent of rhyming slang (Harry Wraggs – Jags). One of the events on the night was a race for jockeys which he won. Dixie Dean won the race for footballers.

The enclosure was formally opened on 30th September, 1933, when Kilmarnock were the visitors. There was a separate Ladies

AYR UNITED SUPPORTERS' CLUB.

16 Beresford Terrace,

Ayr, 29th May, 1929.

Mr. A. Buchanan,
Secretary, A.U.F.C.
Somerset Road,
Back Hawkhill,
A Y R .

Dear Sir,

The Supporters' Club propose holding a Sports meeting on Glasgow Fair Monday after Race Meeting on that evening, the 15th of July, at 6-45 p.m.

The events are:-
(1) A Football Match, Boxers & Jockeys.
(2) Sprint for Jockeys.
(3) Sprint for Boxers.
(4) Sprint for Footballers.

I was to enquire if the Directors would allow the Sports to be held on Somerset Park on that evening in the interests of sport and of your Club in particular, and will be glad to hear from you at earliest in the matter.

Yours faithfully,

William McClelland
SECRETARY.

The letter requesting permission to stage the sporting event at Somerset Park.

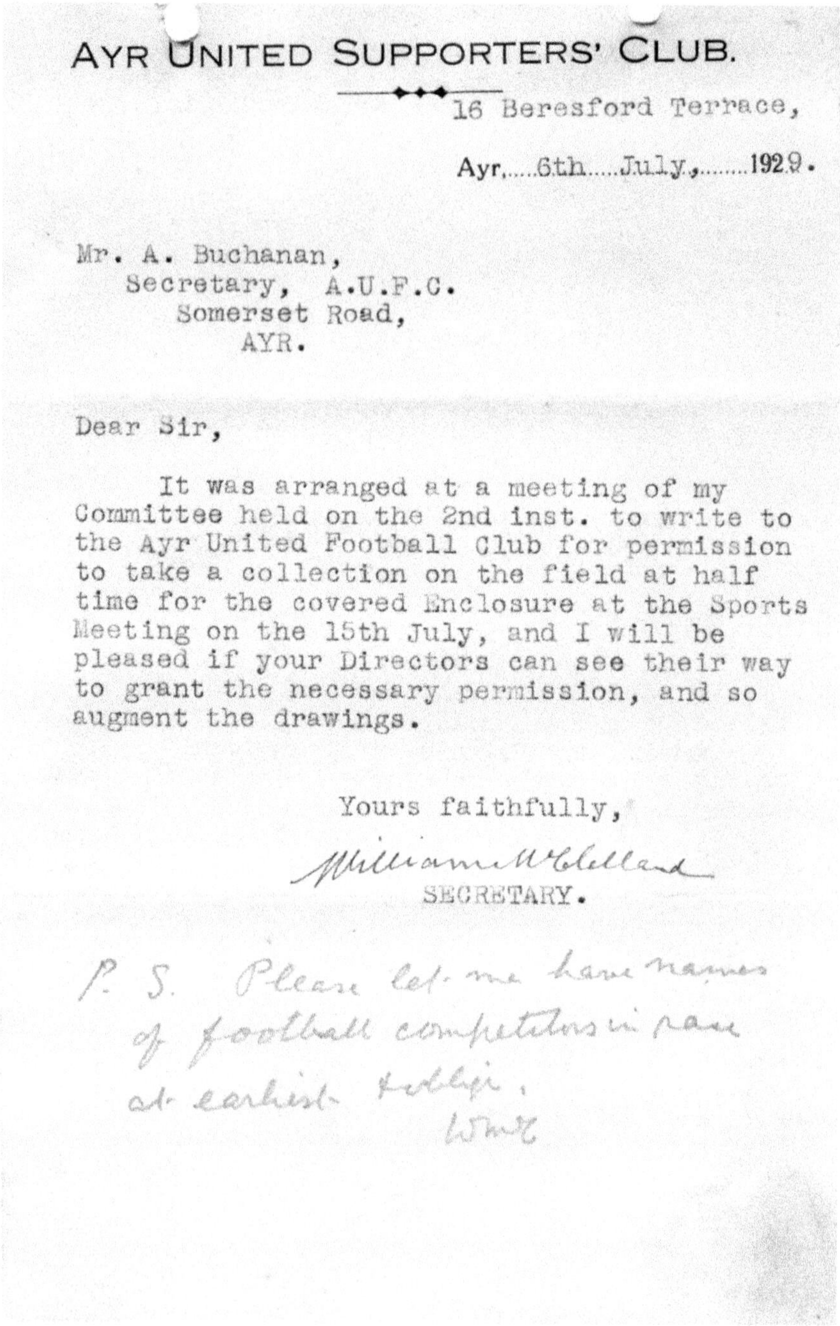

AYR UNITED SUPPORTERS' CLUB.

◆—◆—◆

16 Beresford Terrace,

Ayr,.....6th.....July.,........1929.

Mr. A. Buchanan,
    Secretary, A.U.F.C.
      Somerset Road,
        AYR.

Dear Sir,

    It was arranged at a meeting of my
Committee held on the 2nd inst. to write to
the Ayr United Football Club for permission
to take a collection on the field at half
time for the covered Enclosure at the Sports
Meeting on the 15th July, and I will be
pleased if your Directors can see their way
to grant the necessary permission, and so
augment the drawings.

              Yours faithfully,

              William McClelland
                SECRETARY.

*P. S. Please let me have names
of football competitors in race
at earliest possible.*
          WMcC

Follow-up correspondence requesting permission to rattle some cans

Ayr United Supporters' Club at the time and this body too had contributed to the cost as a result of fund raising efforts. Charles Nair, the architect, executed and gifted the plans.

Jimmy Smith signed for Liverpool on 18th September, 1929, and his local counterpart was Everton centre-forward Dixie Dean. At the conclusion of season 1929/30 they had both scored the same number of goals in the English First Division. That number was twenty-three but Mr Dean had a head start.

Boxers 6 Jockeys 5.

Boxers scorer: McMillan 6

Jockeys scorers: Nevett 2, Wragg, Donoghue, Carr.

Jimmy Smith

THE GOALIE ON THE WING – EPISODE 1

Ayr United versus Cowdenbeath – 19ᵗʰ March, 1932

The heading correctly implies that there were other episodes of similar eccentricity. In the meantime let us embark on the 1932 tale. Victory on this day ensured Ayr United's First Division survival with two games to spare. Billy Brae (5, 15) hit a double and the course of the game indicated that Cowdenbeath would make no inroads on that score. The idyll was disturbed a few minutes before half-time when Bob Hepburn got involved in a collision. He got treatment from Jimmy Dalziel. Dalziel was a trainer who did not fit the stereotype of a bucket and sponge man with a towel over the shoulder. When he was appointed as the Ayr United trainer in 1929 he had already been a certified masseur for fifteen years.

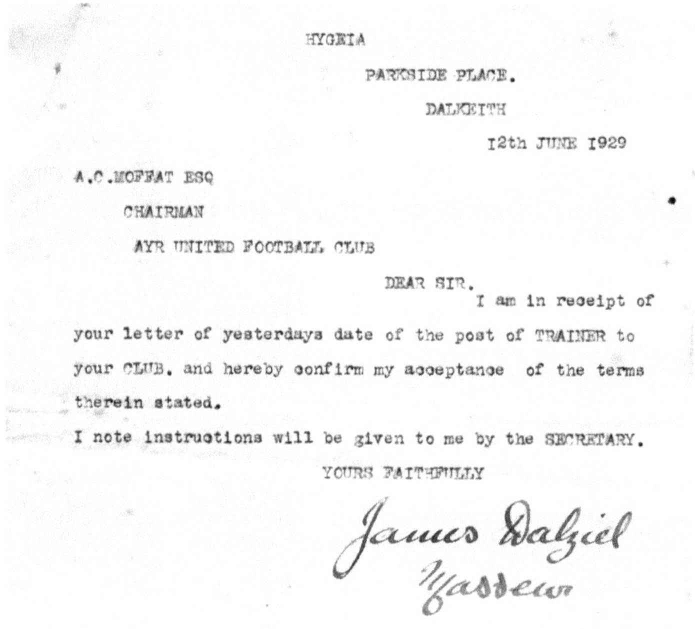

HYGEIA

PARKSIDE PLACE.

DALKEITH

12th JUNE 1929

A.C.MOFFAT ESQ

CHAIRMAN

AYR UNITED FOOTBALL CLUB

DEAR SIR.
                I am in receipt of
your letter of yesterdays date of the post of TRAINER to
your CLUB. and hereby confirm my acceptance   of the terms
therein stated.
I note instructions will be given to me by the SECRETARY.
            YOURS FAITHFULLY

James Dalziel
Masseur

Jimmy Dalziel's letter of acceptance

He was an expert in violet ray treatment and he held the position of chief masseur at a military hospital in Cromarty before going to France during the Great War. At Etaples he was the head of a military electro-therapeutic department. Hepburn undoubtedly had an experienced man tending to him yet the stretcher bearers still had to be called. It was concussion. Centre-half Jimmy McLeod took over in goal. He had previous experience of being an emergency goalkeeper for Ayr United. It happened at Alloa on 9th February, 1926, when he even saved a penalty. Being so close to half-time it can reasonably be imagined that the immediate hope was to hold on to the 2-0 lead until half-time in the hope that 'Hep' would be fit to return after the break, albeit that it was only a ten-minute break back then. What happened next was contrary to expectation. Tommy Robertson had three defenders on him but he still managed to burst through to fire a spectacular goal. The Patna Flyer was living up to his nickname. Not for long though. In the process of making it 3-0 he suffered a knee injury. He got treatment on the touchline then limped to the pavilion. Ayr United finished the first half with nine men including a centre-half in goal. When the second half resumed this increased to ten. Tommy Robertson had his knee bandaged but with the game underway he was seen to be limping on his right wing beat. Five minutes after the restart Hepburn reappeared in a black and white jersey and he took up the outside-left position. On one wing we had a winger limping with an injured knee and on the other wing we had a concussed goalkeeper! It all became even more strange when Hepburn laid on a goal for Alex Merrie. From the crowd perspective the main hero was Jimmy McLeod who created delight by using goalkeeping techniques which were far from textbook. He stayed unbeaten. Alex Merrie scored again to make it 5-0.

The season was played out with a 1-1 draw away to Hearts and another 5-0 home win, against Clyde. Merrie was the only ever present in season 1931/32, scoring twenty-seven goals in the thirty-eight league fixtures. There had only been one previous instance of an Ayr United player scoring more in a First Division league season. That was Jimmy Richardson with twenty-nine in season 1914/15.

Ayr United 5 Cowdenbeath 0. First Division.

Team: Hepburn, Willis, Fleming, Taylor, McLeod, McCall, Robertson, Smith, Merrie, Brannan and Brae.

Scorers: Billy Brae 2, Tommy Robertson, Alex Merrie 2.

GALE FORCE EPISODE 1

Ayr United versus Partick Thistle – 19th October, 1935

The Scottish race has a tendency to be very practical. Rather than ponder on the capacity for severe destruction brought about by severe winds we can expect a more optimistic sentiment: "At least it's a good drying day". This is tempered by the further observation that, on 19th October, 1935, any washing hung out to dry in Ayr would have been blown to Arran or beyond. In the columns of the *Glasgow Herald* there was a summary of just how destructive the wind was in Ayr on that day. Gusts were typically measured at 75mph but, when conditions were at their worst, 84mph was recorded.

"Property suffered extensively in Ayr, the gale being the most violent experienced for a generation. The streets were littered with chimney cans and slates. A large chimney in North Harbour Street seemed likely to collapse and tenants were moved from neighbouring properties. At Wellington Square a large piece of masonry crashed into a tearoom. A large section of the roof of the covered terracing at Somerset Park was blown off. At a riding school at Belmont half of the corrugated iron roof was swept away and a glass roof at Newton Gas Works was destroyed. Two buses arriving in Ayr had their roofs blown off. There were exceptionally high tides and huge waves swept over the esplanade. A small yacht, owned by local men, was swamped at her moorings near the slip dock and a motor boat in the river also went down."

Let us cherry-pick from that report. Ayr's most violent gale in a generation! Destruction to the Railway End roof at Somerset Park! Buses with their roofs blown off! That latter point is particularly thought provoking.

Ayr United versus Partick Thistle on the same day – game on! Partick Thistle won the toss and, quite naturally, their captain elected to take wind advantage in the first half. Conditions were so bad that the Stand was expected to be unoccupiable. Impulsively or otherwise it did get opened. The Ayr goalkeeper was T.G. Smith, otherwise known as Gregg Smith. His initials denoted his amateur status. In the previous month he had been signed from Queen's Park at which club he struggled to get a first team game due to the form of Desmond White, a future Celtic chairman. In the early stages it was apparent that Gregg Smith's goalkicks were actually a goal threat. Farcically he was taking goalkicks then diving back in case he had to save his own kick. Some of his kicks resulted in corners for Partick Thistle. Elaborate build-ups by the opposition worked to Ayr's advantage. Direct action could have been a lot more damaging. In total defiance of the elements Ayr United took the lead in the 19th minute when John Watters scored with a cleverly taken shot. This 1-0 lead was grimly preserved until the half-time whistle.

In the 63rd minute Fally Rodger made it 2-0. This development was a great relief because Partick Thistle were contriving to play better football against the wind. Tension crept in when Partick got a penalty, the award of which aroused the ire of the crowd. The ire increased a notch when Stuart Calderwood converted it. This perceived injustice was corrected with three minutes to go. Penalty to Ayr! Andy McCall did the needful and time was soon called on a 3-1 win.

It was then time to head for home while taking care to traipse over fallen chimney pots and keep an eye skyward for falling masonry. The wiser fans would already have battened down the hatches before heading out.

Ayr United 3 Partick Thistle 1. First Division.

Team: T.G. Smith, Dyer, Bourhill, Taylor, Watson, Holland, Watters, McCall, Fisher, Dimmer and Rodger.

Scorers: John Watters, Fally Rodger, Andy McCall.

THE GOALIE ON THE WING – EPISODE 2

Partick Thistle versus Ayr United – 7ᵗʰ March, 1936

The goalie on the wing in this tale has Bob Hepburn as the main character in common with the similar tale of woe you will have read from 1932. Substitutes in Scottish football would not be adopted for thirty more years but this match from 1936 was a good argument for such a system.

Bob Hepburn

Ayr United went to Firhill as the bottom-placed club in the First Division. The fight to stay up was far from a lost cause by the first Saturday in March. It was tightly packed at the foot yet the vital quest for points was all too apparent. The four ex-Partick Thistle players in the Ayr team were in familiar environs. They were Hugh Baigrie, Fred Pope, John Wylie and John Torbet. By laying constant siege to the Partick goal in the first half hour it could easily have been misconstrued that Ayr United were the team in the top half of the table. That pressure brought the reward of a John Wylie goal but the lead looked fragile when goalkeeper Bob Hepburn got stretchered off with a head injury ten minutes before half-time. While he was getting three stitches inserted his goalkeeping deputy was right-back Jimmy Dyer. It is quite obvious that Dyer was hoping that he would be relieved of his goalkeeping duties at half-time. It was a forlorn hope. Early in the second half Hepburn did come back on but any pretence at a return to normality quickly vanished when he played on the left wing. Dyer made the best of a bad situation. He defended the Ayr United goal with the assurance of an experienced goalkeeper. Could his luck hold? In time he was beaten. Robert Regan equalised (70) then put Partick Thistle ahead (80). At this point Hepburn resumed his goalkeeping duties. This was medically insane in an age when goalkeepers were afforded little protection. Yet it transpired into a tactical masterstroke when John Torbet equalised with two minutes to go.

For the following Saturday's visit from Dundee the goalkeeper was Gregg Smith who sacrificed an amateur international appearance to play. That match was lost 2-1 to a goal in the last minute. Smith was retained for one more match, a 1-0 win away to Hibs.

Bob Hepburn's misadventure and that of Jimmy Dyer captured little newspaper coverage in comparison to the major story occurring on the same date. Hitler sent his troops into the Rhineland in a clear contravention of the Treaty of Versailles. The risk of war was beginning to develop.

Partick Thistle 2 Ayr United 2. First Division.

Team: Hepburn, Dyer, Strain, Baigrie, Currie, Holland, Pope, Wylie, McGibbons, Steele and Torbet.

Scorers: John Wylie, John Torbet.

THE FIVE JOCKS

Third Lanark versus Ayr United – 24ᵗʰ April, 1936

Many flamboyant names have appeared on Ayr United team sheets throughout the years. We have had names like Niclas Nylen, Claudio Valetta, Laurent D'jaffo, Luc Sonor, Kristjan Finnbogason, Jean Francois Peron, Jean-Yves Anis, Rocky Visconte and Farid El Alagui. This is just a brief selection and the purpose of the exercise is to contrast these names with those in the Ayr United dressing room in 1936.

The match highlighted here was a Friday night fixture against Third Lanark at Cathkin Park. On the previous Saturday a 6-0 defeat at Celtic Park meant that the chance of escaping relegation was highly improbable. In order for it to happen it was necessary to beat Third Lanark in the final fixture then hope that Clyde would lose their last two games and Airdrie would lose their remaining game. The fantasy did not materialise and relegation did occur but we are beginning to stray off the topic. Let us return to the subject of players' names. On the night of that final match there were no players in the visiting dressing with flash Christian names like Laurent, Jean-Yves or Farid and there was certainly no one who would have answered to the name of Rocky. All except one of the five Ayr forwards had the name John, albeit that this was sometimes commuted to Jock. John Holland was in the half-back line thereby taking the quota of Johns to five. What of the rest? The remainder of the team comprised two called Davy, one called Hugh (Shug in the Scottish vernacular) one Jimmy, one Terry and one Gregg. The latter was the goalkeeper who was always listed as T.G. Smith, his initials denoting his amateur status, but he got called by his middle name. His previous club, almost inevitably, was Queen's Park. Two nights before the Third Lanark game he had played for Scotland in an amateur international in Belfast.

On the previous Saturday the home team had lost 1-0 to Rangers in the Scottish Cup final, Hampden being located a short walk from their own ground. The crowd was 88,859. Would Third Lanark suffer

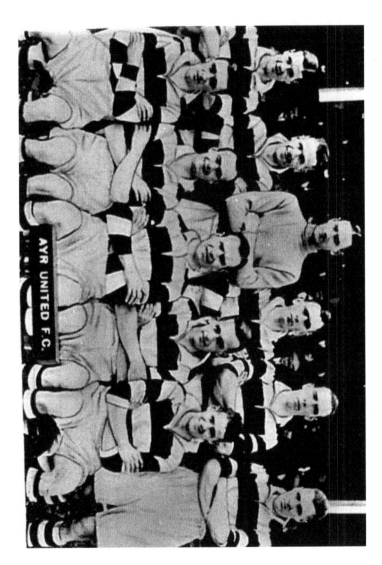

Ayr United FC 1935/36

an adverse reaction due to a sense of anti-climax? If so, it did not show. John Wylie scored for Ayr in the 12th minute but by half-time the deficit was 3-1, Morrison, Gallagher and Geordie Hay having scored. Kennedy made it an almost unassailable 4-1 although Jock Taylor pulled one back. Hay then Kennedy extended it to 6-2. With relegation certain and the pressure relieved the Ayr team managed to catch its second wind. Jock Taylor then John Torbet with a penalty put a semi-respectable veneer on the defeat at 6-4.

Bert Bell wrote an excellent history of Third Lanark. It was entitled *Still Seeing Red* and it was published in 1996. The back cover of the book mentions that Bert was taken to the 1936 Scottish Cup final by an uncle. We will never know whether the same uncle took him to the Ayr United game at Cathkin Park on the following Friday night. If so he would have seen a ten-goal epic resulting in Ayr United's relegation as the bottom club.

On the next day Clyde beat Queen of the South 3-0 at Shawfield and Airdrie drew 1-1 at Arbroath. Clyde therefore narrowly escaped the drop and Airdrie went down as the second bottom club.

Season 1936/37 brought a glorious romp to the Second Division title with some club records being broken in the process. New signings were made. Those included Jock Newall and Jock Mayes. If you had wandered into an Ayr United training session in 1936 and shouted out the name Jock you could be sure that more than a few heads would have turned round.

Third Lanark 6 Ayr United 4. First Division.

Team: T.G. Smith, Dyer, Strain, Baigrie, Currie, Holland, Taylor, Wylie, McGibbons, Steele and Torbet.

Scorers: John Wylie, Jock Taylor 2, John Torbet.

Fally Rodger faced an ordeal at Celtic Park in 1940. He is shown here on a less turbulent day in 1932/33. The team mate on the right is William McGrath.

THE TEAM THAT PICKED ITSELF

Celtic versus Ayr United – 13th January, 1940

Selection difficulties during wartime were expected. When the Second World War was declared the contracts of the Ayr United players were cancelled in line with an instruction from the Scottish Football Association. Their full time contracts got replaced by part time contracts at £2 per week. In the months ahead military demands took priority as a growing succession of players got called up. There was important work to be done too whether in the shipyards or engagement in employment clandestinely defined as being "of national importance". By January 1940 manager Frank Thompson was adept at coping with personnel problems. However with a Regional League game at Celtic Park fast approaching there were genuine concerns about getting a team on the field. Left-half Jock Newall had played his last match for the club in a 3-3 draw at Motherwell the Saturday before. He had been called up by the Royal Engineers and he was to become the only Ayr United player involved in the evacuation of Dunkirk. It took Mr Thompson until the night before the match to get a replacement. This was William Sneddon of Swansea Town who was conveniently stationed in the area. At short notice James Hall and Jock Whiteford both called off with flu. Hall being a goalkeeper, this posed an especially awkward dilemma. It was Friday night! Mr Thompson phoned Donald Turner, his Partick Thistle counterpart. Mr Turner obligingly agreed that Bobby Johnstone could play for Ayr the next day. Partick's home game against St. Mirren was already postponed. It hardly mattered that this was the same Bobby Johnstone who had played in goal for Partick Thistle when his team lost 7-0 at Somerset Park the month before. On the next morning the Ayr United party alighted at Central Station and, as good as his word, Mr Turner was there with his goalkeeper. Immediately there was a three-cornered confab which looked ominously like a hitch. It was a hitch! For reasons which were not made public Johnstone could not or would not play.

Tommy Robertson

The problems mounted on arrival at Celtic Park. Centre-forward Jacky 'Elkie' Clark, who had netted a hat-trick at Motherwell the week before, had not arrived. He was a key player having scored seventeen Regional League goals so far. Clark had a good reason. He was a bricklayer who had been working a shift that morning. His work finished at 1pm, just one hour before kick-off. With little to spare he managed to get there on time. Mr Thompson's relief was only partial. He was in a dressing room of players with no goalkeeper. Then came what seemed to be an answer to a prayer. Former Ayr United goalkeeper Bob Smith, then of Dundee United, looked into the Ayr dressing room. He lived in Greenock and his last game for Ayr United had been on Christmas Day 1937. It was interesting too that he was at Celtic Park. At this time he was just two months away from signing for Celtic. His rendezvous with old friends was secondary to the more pressing priority of getting him changed into his kit. On a day such as this there just had to be another problem.

It was too late to register him even as a loan player. Mr Thompson then considered three options for a replacement goalkeeper. These were right-back Jimmy Dyer, centre-half Davy Currie and outside-left Fally Rodger. Quite why he chose the latter can only be guessed at. It would have been a desperate measure either way.

There were eleven players precisely, hence the heading 'The Team That Picked Itself'. Davy Currie was switched from left-back to centre-half to replace the absent Jock Whiteford. Until Whiteford's arrival in the summer of 1939 Currie had been the regular centre-half anyway. Jimmy Dyer was switched from right-back to left-back and Jimmy Craik was brought in at right-back. Lewis Thow filled the outside-left position vacated by Fally Rodger. This was Thow's best position.

In the second minute Bobby Hogg fouled Jacky Clark. The resultant free-kick was a yard outside the penalty area. William Sneddon struck it expertly for a great goal. It was a brilliant start to his Ayr United debut. For a makeshift goalkeeper Rodger was inspirational. He dealt with the bombardment on his goal by repelling all the shots that came his way in the first half although the fine detail of some reports told that some of those shots were hitting him when he was unaware. In the 27th minute Johnny Crum was faced with a tap-in from almost on the goal line. Rodger upended him in an act that would see his dismissal in the modern game. Willie Lyon took the penalty and it was saved. In the history of Ayr United there are only three instances of outfield players saving a penalty while acting as an emergency goalkeeper. In addition to this one in 1940 the other instances were Jimmy McLeod at Alloa on 9th February, 1926 and John Robertson away to Dundee on 18th April, 1998. Three minutes before half-time Celtic were left to rue their miss. Tommy Robertson sped past Jock Morrison and crossed for Jacky Clark to make it 2-0 with a low shot. The two Ayr scorers were both formerly of Rutherglen Glencairn. In the 63rd minute it became 3-0. A Lewis Thow cross was partially cleared by goalkeeper Donald McKay to allow Jacky Clark to prod it over the line. Fifteen minutes from the end Johnny Gould scored for Celtic although the visibility was so poor that it took keen eyesight to identify him.

Frank Thompson had a fraught Friday night and Saturday morning. When the final whistle blew at Celtic Park he was at complete ease.

Celtic 1 Ayr United 3. Regional League.

Team: Rodger, Craik, Dyer, Cox, Currie, Sneddon, Robertson, McKenzie, Clark, Hamilton and Thow.

Scorers: William Sneddon, Jacky Clark 2.

HEADS OR TAILS?

Ayr United versus Hamilton Accies – 1ˢᵗ August, 1951

Ayr United have only ever competed in two matches that were decided on the toss of a coin. For the Ayr Charity Cup final at home to Kilmarnock on 12th August, 1931, it was agreed that the number of corner-kicks would be the decider in the event of a draw. It ended 2-2 with each team having won five corners. Then came the toss of a coin which resulted in Ayr United taking custody of the Ayr Charity Cup for the thirteenth time. This was the only historical precedent for what happened in 1951, also on an August evening and also at Somerset Park.

When Ayr United reached the final of the Centenary Cup in 1990 the occasion was widely publicised as Ayr United's first national final but this was factually incorrect. To commemorate the Festival of Britain in 1951 there was a competition called the Festival St. Mungo Quaich. The participating clubs were the 'B' Division clubs therefore the criteria was the same as the Centenary Cup of 1990 since it was competed for by league clubs outwith the top league. It could be argued that neither comprised a major tournament but nevertheless both were national tournaments with a comparable entry criteria. Ayr United beat Cowdenbeath, Stirling Albion and Hamilton Accies all at home. The final was lost 2-1 to Dumbarton after extra time at Firhill. Beating Hamilton Accies in the semi-final was entirely down to luck.

Hamilton captain Walter Rothera won the toss at the start of the match. Fortune then continued to favour his team. They had a 2-0 lead by the 22ⁿᵈ minute and this was still intact at half-time. Ten minutes after half-time Norman Christie converted a penalty. Six minutes afterwards Ross Henderson equalised. It remained in the balance until extra time when the Accies regained the lead. Ian Crawford struck in the 113ᵗʰ minute for 3-3. Then came the coin toss which was a hugely unsuitable way to divide the teams. In days of old the corner-kick count was sometimes taken into

Willie Japp

account although not in major cup matches. There is criticism of the more modern method of a shootout yet that is beyond reproach in comparison to the primitive act of a coin toss. Observant spectators may have noticed something obscure that was potentially relevant. As mentioned previously Walter Rothera won the toss for Hamilton at the kick-off. At the start of extra time he won it again. This could open up a debate on the subject of probability. It could equally be argued that the chance of it landing heads or tails is 50/50 regardless of what has happened before. Luck rather than science would decide. Norrie McNeil guessed correctly. It was an Ayr "win". The use of punctuation is merely replicating how it was reported back then.

Luck was a scarce commodity in the final on the Monday evening of the following week. With the score at 1-1 in extra time Willie Gallagher had a goal disallowed by referee Jack Mowat. The decision induced loud criticism. Bringing the frustration to boiling point was Finnie's winner for Dumbarton in the last minute of extra time. The result was an embarrassment in the context of Dumbarton centre-half Jimmy Whyte having gone off injured after twenty minutes, never to return. They were a man down for 100 minutes.

In suggesting that Ayr United were unlucky it could be argued that the team's quota of luck was exhausted in the semi-final. Nine days later the teams met at Ayr in the league. Dumbarton were beaten 5-0 in an illustration of how games should be won.

There was a third instance of a game at Somerset Park being decided on the toss of a coin. It happened on 23rd May, 1970, when France played East Germany in the semi-final of the European International Youth Tournament. After a 1-1 draw an announcement was made that no extra time would be played. This caused some booing. A coin was tossed from within the precincts of the Stand. The result was in East Germany's favour.

Ayr United 3 Hamilton Accies 3 after extra time. Festival St. Mungo Quaich semi-final.

Team: Round, Leckie, Perrie, Christie, McNeil, Nesbit, Japp, Crawford, Henderson, Gallagher and Cryle.

Scorers: Norman Christie, Ross Henderson, Ian Crawford.

Norman Christie

WHITE FIELD WITH RED LINES

Dundee United versus Ayr United – 19th January, 1952

There is an interesting saying that a trip into the past is like a trip into a foreign country. A trip into this particular day in 1952 would reveal much that is alien to dwellers of the 21st century. Old Firm dominance is a way of life in Scottish football but it certainly wasn't at this time. The season would finish with Hibs as league winners, Motherwell as Scottish Cup winners and Dundee as League Cup winners. By this date in January the six leading league clubs in Scotland were, in order, Hibs, Hearts, East Fife, Rangers, Raith Rovers and Queen of the South. Albeit that the season was so far advanced, Celtic sat thirteenth, just two points above the relegation zone. Ayr United and Dundee United sat third and fourth respectively in 'B' Division. The top two of Clyde and Falkirk looked catchable therefore Dundee United versus Ayr United was a fixture brimming with importance.

There was an inch of snow on the Tannadice pitch. Referee William Brittle was happy to let the game go ahead. At this time it did not justify a postponement provided that the ground underneath was not too hard. Football played on a carpet of snow was not a peculiar sight to the football fan of 1952. The convention was simply to clear the lines in it. True to that convention the Dundee United groundsman had cleared the appropriate channels in the grass. Rather than leave it at that he then marked the regulation lines with red oxide. It was beautiful and distinctive. On a regular Saturday it would be a green pitch with white markings. It was now a white pitch with red markings.

A stranger in the Ayr team was goalkeeper John Petrie. He had been freed by Third Lanark and manager Archie Anderson obtained his signature on the morning of the match. This was to prove his only first team game for Ayr United.

The field may have been of Christmas-card-esque beauty but it was dangerous. Mike McKenna pulled a muscle before he had even

John Petrie

kicked a ball. He went off to get his thigh strapped but his return to the fray was futile. Norrie McNeil, his captain, instructed him to retire from the game. Note that the captain rather than the manager had the responsibility for such decisions. Ayr United were now a man down for the remainder of the match and the home team capitalised on their numerical superiority by taking the lead when George Grant beat Petrie with a header. In the 25th minute a Willie Japp cross was met by goalkeeper Bob Wylie who punched it against team mate Bobby Ross and it fell for Jimmy Baker to draw Ayr level. Five minutes beyond the break Frank Quinn seized onto a long pass then beat Petrie for 2-1 to the home team. Willie Japp concluded the scoring at 2-2 in the 67th minute. It was a good result with ten men.

The *Ayr Advertiser* report commented: "This Saturday Ayr United will be back at Dundee to tackle the city's big team." The "city's big team" was Dundee and the team had to retrace the journey for a first round Scottish Cup tie. Snow was still lying in the city. Clearing the Dens Park pitch of snow must have been considered too much of an undertaking. Only the six-yard areas were cleared whereupon they were sprinkled with sand. The home team played in specially adapted rubber boots and won 4-0, the same score they would ultimately lose by in the final against Motherwell. It was a duller spectacle in the absence of the red oxide lines favoured by their neighbours.

Dundee United 2 Ayr United 2 'B' Division.

Team: Petrie, Henderson, McKeown, Fraser, McNeil, Nesbit, Japp, Robertson, Baker, Harper and McKenna.

Scorers: Jimmy Baker, Willie Japp.

TEA IS SERVED

Ayr United versus Queen's Park – 3rd May, 1952

The Ayr Charity Cup has a very noble history. It was first competed for in 1885 and there were high hopes that that the inaugural competition would be won by the local club Ayr FC. The other participating clubs were Hurlford, Mauchline, Kilwinning Monkcastle, Lugar Boswell, Cumnock, Annbank and Kilmarnock. After beating Kilwinning Monkcastle 7-2 there was great disappointment when Ayr FC lost 3-1 at home to Lugar Boswell. Well it would be at home since all of the ties were played in Ayr. In true 1880s style a protest was lodged. Luckily this protest was upheld and Kilmarnock were beaten 5-2 in the Beresford Park final. At the end the players were carried off the field by the joyful fans. The trophy presentation took place in the Council Chambers that evening. That was after both teams had tea in the Ayrshire and Galloway. On the previous Saturday the teams had contested the Kilmarnock Charity Cup final at Rugby Park. That was the occasion of a 3-2 win for Ayr FC.

Several decades into the future the Ayr Charity Cup had a much leaner look with just two contestants. It was commuted to a straight final between Ayr United and either Kilmarnock or Queen's Park. Due to the gathering war clouds the 1939 final did not get played and in the immediate post war years there was no resumption of the Ayr Charity Cup but in 1952 it got revived to commemorate the 750th anniversary of Ayr becoming a Royal Burgh. Pedantically it may be pointed out that historians had got the date wrong. Ayr's royal charter had been granted in 1205, not 1202 as originally thought. Queen's Park visited for the 1952 final. It was supposed to be a one-off revival of the competition. It is true that this was the last final but it would have been played in 1953 had not Queen's Park been unavailable through a Glasgow Cup commitment.

Silver tea services had been purchased in anticipation of being presented to the 1939 winners. For thirteen years these tea services had sat in a bank vault but they saw daylight when it was decided to award them to the 1952 winners. In those austere times it was a quite wonderful prize. Indeed even in more prosperous times it would have been a wonderful prize. It was a real touch of class.

In the 17th minute Jimmy Inglis got to an Alex Beattie cross and beat the challenge of goalkeeper Morton Ramsay for 1-0. Derek Grierson's equaliser made it a marathon afternoon with extra time. Grierson was at the end of his Queen's Park career since he was on the point of signing for Rangers. Ten minutes into extra time Ian Crawford hit the winner. The Ayr Charity Cup remains a handsome adornment to the Ayr United boardroom because it has since remained uncontested.

It must have been a cluttered home dressing room with each player having been presented with a silver tea service. Your writer used to visit Jacky Robertson occasionally in his retirement years. His beautiful prize from 1952 still adorned the sideboard in his Prestwick home.

The original premise of the Ayr Charity Cup was to generate funds for Ayr County Hospital. However the money handed over was net of some considerable expenditure. In 1885 that expenditure was in respect of medals, teas, field rent, railway fares, printing and bill posting, police, referees, umpires (linesmen), footballs, the purchase of a leather bag, groundsman's fees, secretarial expenses and inscribing the silver plate on the base of the cup. The 1952 prize would have been expensive but it had all been paid for in 1939.

Ayr United 2 Queen's Park 1 after extra time. Ayr Charity Cup.

Team: Round, Fraser, McKeown, Cairns (Leckie), McNeil, Robertson, Japp, Crawford, Inglis, Hutton and Beattie.

Note that Sam Leckie went on as a substitute for the injured Bobby Cairns. This was unconventional for 1952.

Scorers: Jimmy Inglis, Ian Crawford.

THE WHITE BALL

Ayr United versus Queen's Park – 22ⁿᵈ November, 1952

This was a typical Scottish winter's day. Roads were icy and there was a veil of mist. The big match on the football calendar was East Fife versus Hibs. It was the 'A' Division leaders versus the second-placed club. Hibs, who had been the league champions in each of the two previous seasons, won the match to close the gap at the top. The leaders in 'B' Division were Stirling Albion. Ayr United entered the day in third place but a win over Queen's Park caused a shift into second place because Hamilton Accies only drew at home to Kilmarnock who sat fourth from the bottom. With there being two automatic promotion places this was an exciting development.

Before the game at Ayr kicked-off there was a great novelty. The ball was white! Football had been played at Somerset Park for more than sixty-four years and this was the first time a white ball had been used at the ground. The uniform colour had always been brown. There had to be a reason for such a radical change. The rationale was that the white ball would be more visible in the mist. It is an argument which may have been open to debate but the decision was made. It was so revolutionary that the *Evening Times* report mentioned it in the first sentence. "Queen's kicked-off with a white ball."

In the first half Queen's Park goalkeeper Hastie Weir saw a lot more of the white sphere than he would have liked. In the 16ᵗʰ minute he came running out for a ball and the race was on between him and Willie Japp. Being endowed with greater speed Japp got there first and he easily shot into the empty goal. On the half-hour mark Mike McKenna crossed for Jacky Robertson to touch it past Weir for 2-0. That lead was doubled within the last two minutes of the first half. A shot from Joe Hutton got palmed out in the direction of Willie Japp who availed himself of the opportunity. Then, before the game had settled down again, Joe Hutton scored with an exquisite drive from twenty yards. The half-time score of 4-0 was ultimately the final result. It was the seventh of eight consecutive league wins.

One week later the Albion Rovers versus Ayr United match got abandoned after twenty-one minutes due to fog. Reports touched extensively on the cause of the abandonment but none of them referred specifically to a white ball so we can assume it was a traditional brown one with the equally traditional lace. Younger fans will have been regaled with tales of how the old traditional football would absorb moisture and could be compared with a medicine ball on a rainy day. The medicine ball comparison was a bit of an exaggeration but it was not a totally ridiculous comparison. In contrast the white footballs of today are synthetic and shed moisture. Footwear has developed accordingly. The old Manfield Hotspur boots, universally favoured in the 1950s, were exceptionally sturdy and afforded ankle protection. Modern boots are apt to draw a lazy comparison with carpet slippers but they are more adept for mobility and comfort.

Ayr United 4 Queen's Park 0. 'B' Division.

Team: Round, Thomson, Leckie, Willie Fraser, McNeil, Nesbit, Japp, Robertson, Jim Fraser, Hutton and McKenna.

Scorers: Willie Japp 2, Jacky Robertson, Joe Hutton.

Willie Fraser

GALE FORCE EPISODE 2

Ayr United versus St. Johnstone – 31st January, 1953

Gale Ruled The Game

Ayr United 5 St Johnst'ne 2

In this phase of history the strength of the wind was never taken into account as a reason for postponing a football match. The criteria narrowed down to a playable pitch and proper visibility. Even frost-bound pitches were commonly deemed to be playable. On this particular day Somerset Park was eminently playable and there was not even a hint of fog. The question of a postponement was not even discussed but in the modern day the wind factor would have put paid to the fixture with no deliberation. Football played in high winds is a farcical spectacle. There is the illusion that they are playing with a beach ball. Today the issue of spectator safety is a prime consideration. Sometimes this principle is too rigidly applied. Why postpone a match when the only apparent danger is flying crisp packets?

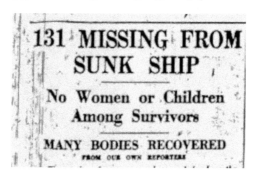

131 MISSING FROM SUNK SHIP

No Women or Children Among Survivors

MANY BODIES RECOVERED

FROM OUR OWN REPORTERS

On 31st January, 1953, the wind was so extreme that there were disastrous consequences and this is not meant in a footballing context. Crippled by mountainous seas in an 80-mile-per-hour gale, the Stranraer to Larne ferry sank. There were 128 passengers on board as well as fifty to sixty crew members (there were conflicting reports). Only forty-four survived, one of whom was former Ayr United player Bert Harper, who was travelling from his New Cumnock home to Belfast to play for Linfield. He made history on 23rd February, 1946, when he scored for Ayr United at Dumbarton. It was the club's first ever goal in the League Cup.

Apart from the spectators having to hold on to their hats the main concern at the outset of St. Johnstone's visit was who would win the toss. Luckily Norrie McNeil won and this meant that he had the choice of ends or kick-off. There was never the remotest possibility that he was going to forfeit the choice of ends in favour of having the kick-off. Wind advantage was huge and there was a hope that it would subside by the second half. In the ninth minute a free-kick from Willie Fraser was met by Bobby Cairns who slammed it high into the net from eighteen yards. Goalkeeper George Brown would already have known that he was facing a busy shift until half-time. Two minutes later he had to retrieve the ball from the net again. A corner-kick was played to Willie Fraser who scored with a ferocious shot from twenty-five yards. Seven minutes later Gerry Tracy dribbled the ball round the stranded Brown and gleefully netted goal number three. After six more minutes had elapsed Brown did well to save from Mike McKenna but he could not hold the ball and Tracy made it 4-0. Even with just twenty-four minutes played the game would have been as good as won on another day. Yet the wind showed no sign of easing and the second half was definitely going to be formidable. Nine minutes before the break centre-half Johnny Innes conceded an own goal when he deflected a shot from McKenna. 5-0 by the 36th minute – the question of whether it would be enough still persisted.

With the gale in their favour Dick Andrew scored for St. Johnstone just five minutes into the second half. One minute later Len Round pulled off a superb save from Peter Armit. It really was now a matter of trying to cling on. For the first ten minutes of the second half the ball did not even cross the halfway line. Corner-kicks were particularly difficult to defend. This was proven with half an hour left when the ball came over and Dave Forsyth scored with a header, albeit that a conflicting report judged it to be an own goal. 5-2 – there was cause for worry. The gale would not abate. Could Ayr United beat the clock? No further scoring occurred but the Ayr United goal remained threatened to the end.

The *Ayr Advertiser* headline summarised it neatly:

Winning The Toss Was Vital In This Storm-Swept Match.

One week later Ayr United won 5-1 at Buckie in the second round of the Scottish Cup. There was a two-minutes silence for the victims of the stricken vessel The Princess Victoria. Coincidentally the venue was Victoria Park.

Ayr United 5 St. Johnstone 2. 'B' Division.

Team: Round, Leckie, Rodger, Fraser, McNeil, Cairns, Japp, McKeown, Tracy, Finnie and McKenna.

Scorers: Bobby Cairns, Willie Fraser, Gerry Tracy 2, Johnny Innes own goal.

En route to Buckie on 7th February, 1953.
Left to right: Norrie McNeil, Alan Rodger, Gordon Finnie, Gerry Tracy,
Jacky Robertson, Jimmy O'Neil (trainer) and Sam Leckie. On the train:
Bobby Cairns (front) and Len Round (back).

Queen's Park versus Ayr United almost a year later, this time with a brown ball! The date is 31st October, 1953. The goalkeeper is Len Round. Norrie McNeil is far left. Sam Leckie (3) and Alan Rodger are covering the posts. The Queen's Park player is Max Murray and the referee is Bobby Davidson.

A SLEDGEHAMMER TO CRACK A NUT

Ayr United versus Airdrie – 27ᵗʰ October, 1956

This game resulted in a comfortable home win but it still had disciplinary repercussions for the club. It was the Saturday after losing 6-1 at home to Aberdeen. Understandably Jacky Cox made changes and these were relatively sweeping. In goal Len Round replaced Willie Travers. At right-back Bobby Bell replaced Alex Paterson. Peter Price came in for Willie Paton at centre-forward and Paton, in turn, took Bobby Stevenson's place at inside-right. At outside-left Matt Murray made way for Alex Beattie. Older readers may ponder why Price and Beattie did not play in the Aberdeen match. In reports of injuries within the squad neither were mentioned. Peter Price once told the author that he did not always have a good relationship with Jacky Cox and that his favourite Ayr United manager was "Auld Neilly" (Neil McBain). He also mentioned that he liked playing against his cousin, Billy Price. It happened in this match.

Airdrie took a 28ᵗʰ minute lead from a player who did his training at Somerset Park. The scorer was Willie 'Cowboy' McCulloch. In future years he would render fine service to Ayr United as an assistant trainer. Four minutes before half-time a Willie Japp free-kick was mis-handled by goalkeeper Dave Walker and Peter Price nodded the equaliser. Eleven minutes after the break a Willie Japp corner was played on by Willie Paton for Peter Price to score with another header. His hat-trick of headers was completed four minutes later. A quite brilliant strike from Willie Japp put the seal on it at 4-1.

Peter Price's hat-trick of headers should have been the main story. It was the first time in Ayr United's history that a player had achieved this feat. Since then only Eddie Moore (twice) and Ian McAllister have done this. However the story that did develop was in relation to an incident that very few of the crowd were aware of and the assembled media seemed oblivious of. According to the referee's report a spectator had thrown a nut at him. This was deemed to be so serious that the matter was to be raised at a meeting of the Referee

He was an opponent in 1956 but here we see Willie 'Cowboy' McCulloch in 1984 retiring as assistant trainer to Ayr United.

Willie McCulloch, far left, alongside trainer Willie Wallace. The players are Billy Paton then Ian Campbell.

Committee scheduled for 26th November. Even with the benefit of hindsight it is perhaps wrong to heap ridicule on this course of action yet the disciplinary proceedings did seem harsh when put into context. Somerset Park has a history of documented cases of crowd disorder dating back to Victorian times, these transgressions being considerably more serious than throwing a nut. The further action was a clear case of using a sledgehammer to crack a nut (pun intended!).

The minutes of the meeting contained the following: "A missile throwing incident at the Ayr v Airdrieonians game at Somerset Park on October 27th was noted by the committee."

The committee also instructed Ayr United to publish a warning in the match programme. This warning was duly inserted in the programme for the visit of East Fife on 8th December, 1956. Here is the wording that appeared under a heading of Club Notes. It was published in bold print.

> **"At a meeting of the Referee Committee of the Scottish Football Association, Ayr United were instructed to insert a notice in the official programme warning spectators of possible consequences to the club should further offences be committed of the nature of that which occurred in the Ayr United v Airdrieonians game at Somerset Park on 27th October. On that occasion a spectator threw a nut at the referee. The thrower of the nut has not been identified."**

The statement can be qualified with the additional information that the thrower of the nut remained unidentified. After the passage of so much time we can be safe in the knowledge that the perpetrator has successfully escaped detection.

Ayr United 4 Airdrie 1. First Division.

Team: Round, Bell, Thomson, Traynor, Gallagher, Haugh, Japp, Paton, Price, McMillan and Beattie.

Scorers: Peter Price 3, Willie Japp.

Willie Paton

THE CUP WINNING JERSEYS

Ayr United versus Airdrie – 27ᵗʰ February, 1960

Your writer will always remember meeting Peter Price for the first time. He remains Ayr United's greatest player of all time and it was a thrill when he agreed that I could go to his flat for an interview. It wasn't an interview in the rapid question and answer style but more of a pleasant conversation about his Ayr United career. On that evening he produced some photographs, one of which was bewildering. It showed Peter in action at Somerset Park and he was wearing a St. Mirren shirt. It was not merely a black and white striped shirt. The St. Mirren badge could not be mistaken. He could not recall why Ayr United were playing in borrowed kit. However with further research the story emerged.

The club's Scottish Cup run started at Peebles. It was a tie twice postponed due to the pitch having a blanket of snow which had frozen solid. Peebles Rovers requested to forfeit ground rights but the SFA declined the request. It therefore went ahead at their Whitestone Park ground on a Monday afternoon. There was no terracing and it had a little Stand that would have accommodated about 250. The home team could not remotely match First Division Ayr United. It was a 6-1 rout and our share of the gate was a mere £22.

The third round ties took place the following Saturday. Airdrie at Ayr had the promise to be a real Scottish Cup tie in contrast to the shooting practice at Peebles. An SFA ruling dictated that, in the event of a colour clash in a Scottish Cup tie, both teams would have to change their strips. Ayr boss Jacky Cox was not only mindful of this, he had already made preparations. In January he had ordered a set of royal blue jerseys just in case the club would be affected by the ruling. It looked as if it was a very wise precaution in view of the impending Airdrie tie. Then, on checking with Airdrie boss Willie Steel, Mr Cox discovered that their change shirts were sky blue. Let us recap. Both teams played in predominantly white shirts so the ruling compelled both to change. The respective change kits were

OFFICIAL PROGRAMME
1959-60

SATURDAY, 27th FEBRUARY
Scottish Cup—3rd Round   Kick-off 3 p.m.

AYR   UNITED
FOOTBALL AND   ATHLETIC CLUB

SCOTTISH   LEAGUE

FIRST   DIVISION

versus
Airdrieonians

Lucky   N⁰   349

3D   **3**D

3D   **3**D

76

merely different shades of blue. Another colour clash! Mr Cox then had a browse at Somerset Park and he managed to find a variety of old kits but he did not like any of them. Then he phoned St. Mirren boss Willie Reid and he politely requested to borrow a set of jerseys. The borrowed jerseys were the same ones St. Mirren had been wearing when they won the Scottish Cup the year before. That was a good omen. Another good omen was that they had beaten Peebles Rovers on the way to winning the cup. This was the same club Ayr United had vanquished in the round before. It was lucky that St. Mirren had no game on this particular Saturday. At the second round stage they had drawn home and away with Celtic and the second replay was scheduled for the Monday.

This was not the first time Peter Price had worn a St. Mirren shirt. It is not commonly known that St. Mirren was his first senior club. He signed for them from Craigmark Burntonians and was ultimately released before joining Gloucester City. Here in 1960 he scored against sky blue Airdrie in the 25th minute. John McGill headed his team level seven minutes later. In the second half Price wrote his name all over the tie. He completed his hat-trick (54, 60) then Tommy Duncan pulled one back with ten minutes left. Sam McMillan ensured a passage into the quarter-final by making it 4-2 in the last minute. Each goal of Peter Price's hat-trick was taken in quite brilliant fashion. It was a satisfactory afternoon's work and it had been accomplished in disguise.

Not until 16th February, 1974, did an Ayr United player next score a Scottish Cup hat-trick. On that date the feat was achieved by both Davy McCulloch and George McLean in a 7-1 victory at Stranraer.

Ayr United 4 Airdrie 2. Scottish Cup third round.

Team: Hamilton, Burn, Thomson, McIntyre, McLean, Telfer, Fulton, McMillan, Price, Paton and McGhee.

Scorers: Peter Price 3, Sam McMillan.

Peter Price playing for Ayr United in a St. Mirren shirt

3D **3D**

OFFICIAL PROGRAMME

1960-61

SATURDAY, 24th SEPTEMBER
Kick-off 3 p.m.

AYR   UNITED
FOOTBALL AND   ATHLETIC CLUB

SCOTTISH   LEAGUE

FIRST   DIVISION

versus
KILMARNOCK

3D   Lucky № 831   **3D**

THE REFEREE WHO WAS CHEERED OFF

Ayr United versus Kilmarnock – 24th September, 1960

The standside linesman for this match was Jimmy Inglis, a former Ayr United centre-forward. After signing from Queen of the South in February 1952 he made an instant impact. Six league fixtures remained until the end of the season. He struck eight goals in these matches. This was just three behind top scorer Ian Crawford. In 1952/53 the momentum was lost. At the end of October he lost his place having scored one League Cup goal. His next club was Worcester City. Let us recap. This was an Ayrshire derby with a linesman who had an Ayr United connection. Lest there be any thoughts of paranoia you will now be told that the farside linesman was the son of Bob Neave who had been a Kilmarnock player between 1917 and 1922 and was in their Scottish Cup winning team in 1920. Neave senior had also been a league linesman. On 25th November, 1933, he took ill at St.Enoch Station while on the way to run the line at an Ayr United versus Dundee game. His place was taken by a local Junior referee.

The referee for this Ayrshire derby in 1960 was a Mr Stewart from Paisley. Forensic scrutiny would have revealed not even a tenuous connection to either side of the Ayrshire divide. With 17,500 fans in the ground, most of whom were partisan, the referee was potentially a prime target for criticism in a match such as this. Yet the only criticism that would come his way was critical acclaim.

The band of the Scots Guards provided some greatly appreciated pre-match entertainment. Further entertainment was provided seven minutes after the kick-off when Bobby Thomson hit a long free-kick in the direction of the Kilmarnock penalty area. It fell for Killie centre-half Willie Toner who headed it back to goalkeeper Jimmy Brown. The static Brown looked transfixed when the ball entered the net for an own goal. Andy Kerr made it 1-1 twenty minutes later. In the last minute of the first half Alastair McIntyre scored with a shot that Brown got his hands to but could not stop. Alastair's brother Willie was also playing for Ayr United on this day but it is likely that

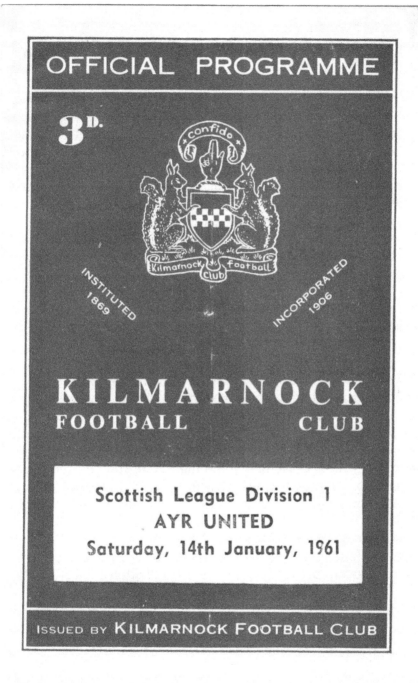

The programme for the return fixture

his concentration was elsewhere. His baby was on the danger list in a Glasgow hospital. Kilmarnock managed to draw level for a second time when right-back Jim Richmond beat Ian Hamilton with a 35-yard wind assisted drive.

The story becomes extraordinary when we look at what happened after time was called on a 2-2 draw. Referee Stewart was cheered off the field by both sets of supporters. The *Ayr Advertiser* report mentioned this as did the *Sunday Post*. Further proof is not needed but here it is anyway. The Ayr United versus Hearts programme of 15th October, 1960, contained the following.

"At the end of our home game against Kilmarnock the supporters of both clubs gave the referee, Mr J. Stewart of Paisley, a rousing ovation as he left the field. We have been asked by Mr Stewart to thank the public for showing their appreciation of his services and to state that he thoroughly enjoyed being in charge of such a sporting game."

Please read that programme excerpt again and during the re-reading remember that we are talking about Ayr United versus Kilmarnock. On the day of the Kilmarnock match the programme editorial implied that there was apt to be some harmony in the football world of 1960.

"None of us wish to see the day when Killie supporters enter one end of the ground and Ayr fans the other. May that day never dawn."

Looking back from six decades later you will well know that there is no longer anything genteel about these fixtures. If couching it in concise terms an apt description nowadays would be 'blood and snotters'. Cynical people may think that the ovation for the referee was an act of sarcasm. It cannot be denied that sarcasm has long been a Scottish trait. On the basis of contemporary reports this notion can be dismissed.

Ayr United 2 Kilmarnock 2. First Division.

Team: Hamilton, Burn, Thomson, Willie McIntyre, Paterson, Walker, Alastair McIntyre, McMillan, Price, Fulton and McGhee.

Scorers: Willie Toner own goal, Alastair McIntyre.

Ian Hamilton

Willie Toner. He scored for Ayr United in 1960 but did not sign for the club until 1963!

BEATEN TWICE ON THE SAME DAY

Ayr United versus Dundee United – 2nd February, 1963

The winter of 1962 trailing into 1963 was awful. Anything you have heard about it will probably be true. The River Ayr was frozen so hard that ice skating took place on it and that is a fact rather than a feeble attempt at sarcasm. After playing Stranraer at Ayr on 8th December, 1962, the club's next home league fixture did not occur until 2nd March, 1963. The only match at Somerset Park between those dates was a Scottish Cup tie against Dundee United. From playing at Forfar on 22nd December until playing away to East Fife on 23rd February, this cup tie was the only game played by Ayr United. Back then matches would go ahead in conditions that would see them immediately postponed today. Yet even by the more relaxed standards of 1962/63 these habitual postponements were necessary. In relation to a league fixture with Albion Rovers scheduled for 19th January manager Neil McBain was asked about the state of Somerset Park. Mr McBain's reply was: "Play football? You could skate on it." In response Bob Blane of the *Ayr Advertiser* went to the ground and he did skate on it. He was a great character.

There was no National Lottery in Britain at this time. The popular get-rich-quick scheme was the football pools. Coupons were distributed with football fixtures and it was a simple matter of ticking off the fixtures anticipated to end in a draw. The premise may have been simple but forecasting eight draws was decidedly difficult. With the game's propensity for the unpredictable it was better to have no knowledge of football and to make the selections blindly. This was a massive industry and the raft of postponements led to a Pools Panel being set up in January 1963. It was the panel's job to decide whether postponed matches would have resulted in a home win, an away win or a draw. For the purpose of the pools their decision was binding and their 'results' were broadcast on television.

Ayr United versus Dundee United was the only Scottish Cup tie played on 2nd February, 1963. Your writer was one of the 4,787

OFFICIAL PROGRAMME

1962 - 63

SCOTTISH CUP—2nd ROUND

SATURDAY, 2nd FEBRUARY

Kick-off 3 p.m.

AYR

FOOTBALL AND

UNITED

ATHLETIC CLUB

SCOTTISH
SECOND

LEAGUE
DIVISION

versus

DUNDEE UN.

Lucky **N⁰** 879

3ᴰ 3ᴰ 3ᴰ 3ᴰ

crowd (technically not due to being lifted over!) and from boyhood recollection you may be told that this match should have been postponed along with the others. The pitch was bone hard. On this particular date the club had a scheduled league fixture away to Queen's Park but it was long known that there was no chance of it proceeding. Nevertheless Queen's Park versus Ayr United was on the list for consideration by the Pools Panel. Maybe we could 'win' that game.

At Somerset Park it was sunny and there was not even a breath of wind but the cold was intense. Jim Irvine (22, 55) put the visitors 2-0 up. Johnny Kilgannon (65) trimmed it to a single-goal deficit and there was intense excitement when decent attempts were made at pursuing an equaliser. Alas we were thwarted by the exceptional form of goalkeeper Sandy Davie. Yet the final whistle brought one consolation. It was then time to return home to the heat of a coal fire.

The Pools Panel decided that Queen's Park versus Ayr United was a 'home win' so, in a manner of speaking, we were beaten twice on the same day. The game was eventually played on the evening of 27th March and the 4-1 home win fully exonerated the panel.

Ayr United 1 Dundee United 2. Scottish Cup 2nd round.

Team: Gallacher, Burn, Milton, Stewart, McGugan, McIntyre, Herron, McMillan, Jones, Kilgannon and McCubbin.

Scorer: Johnny Kilgannon.

Bert McCubbin

THE GOALIE ON THE WING – EPISODE 3

Queen's Park versus Ayr United – 18th January, 1964

This particular goalie-on-the-wing theme differs from the others in the respect that the goalkeeper in question played outfield for the entire match.

One week before the Queen's Park fixture Inverness Thistle had been beaten 3-2 at Ayr in the first round of the Scottish Cup. It was a slender victory against a Highland League club which fielded a 17-year-old goalkeeper as a late deputy. It was far from a stunning success yet great enthusiasm was shown by the home fans at the final whistle. In January 1964 the team was in such a state that even the most minimal cause for celebration was willingly seized upon. At the time of this match against Queen's Park we were fourth from the foot of the Second Division. This translated into being the fourth worst league club in Scotland. Compounding this status was having to live with the sight of Kilmarnock at the top of the First Division table thereby making them Scotland's leading club at the time.

Fifth versus sixteenth in the Second Division was a sporting contest guaranteed to leave vast swathes of empty terracing in the vast bowl that was Hampden Park. The adverse form of the Ayr team was reason enough for most of our own dwindling support to stay at home. As expected the team filed onto the frostbound pitch in silence. Later in the afternoon, to the surprise of no one, the BBC teleprinter spelt out a result of Queen's Park 3 Ayr United 2. Thus far few would have been aware of an unorthodox team selection. In the 1960s there was a Saturday evening ritual in which people would congregate outside newsagents awaiting the delivery of the Evening Times and the Evening Citizen. Both papers were brimful of news of the Saturday afternoon's football action. Browsing either or both of those papers on the way home suddenly became an enlightening experience for Ayr United supporters on the evening of 18th January, 1964. The regular team selection would have shown Johnny Hubbard on the right wing and Kenny Cunningham on the left wing but the

Johnny Kilgannon

player shown as having played on the right wing was Gallacher. The only Gallacher on the club's books was John Gallacher, a goalkeeper. It could not have been a trialist because it was customary to list trialists as 'Newman'. In truth goalkeeper John Gallacher was played at outside-right and it being in the pre-substitute days he played there for the entire game. It was all down to a poverty of resources. He was an emergency replacement for flu victim Johnny Hubbard, the emphasis being on the word 'emergency'. In goal was Alastair Paton, the club's other goalkeeper. Even a cursory glance at the evening newspapers confirmed the unconventional truth. The reports mentioned that the listed Gallacher really was John Gallacher.

Dave Millar, then aged eighteen, scored twice for Queen's Park in the first half, the second of which was from a penalty awarded after Eddie Maxwell had punched the ball out in goalkeeper-style. Three minutes after the break Sandy Jones halved the deficit when he received a pass from Johnny Kilgannon and first-timed it beyond Bobby Clark. After three more minutes had elapsed Jones was fouled inside the box by John Cole. Johnny Kilgannon struck the resultant penalty over the crossbar. Peter Buchanan put Queen's Park 3-1 ahead in the 63rd minute. With fifteen minutes remaining a Sandy Jones header concluded the scoring at 3-2. Gallacher had a quiet match. He retained his place in the team for the following week's Scottish Cup win at Buckie but mercifully he was by then restored to defending the sticks.

It is interesting that the opposition goalkeeper was Bobby Clark. In season 1969/70 he played some first team games for Aberdeen at centre-half. He had lost his place in goal and it was genuinely felt that he was good enough to fill that position.

Queen's Park 4 Ayr United 1. Second Division.

Team: Paton, Grant, Maxwell, Frew, Lindsay, Burn, Gallacher, Kilgannon, Jones, McMillan and Cunningham.

Scorer: Sandy Jones 2.

*John Gallacher in an outfield shirt
— and not for the last time.*

THE IMPOSTER

Ayr United versus East Fife – 27th April, 1966

The heading is probably a little harsh. It has to be admitted that some literary licence has been used. An imposter is someone who pretends to be someone else in order to cheat themself into a situation. This is the tale of a player called John Pullar and there is no evidence that he has ever been guilty of cheating himself into any situation. However the story about to be told will clarify why he had the illusion of being an imposter.

Ayr United faced a punishing run-in to the 1965/66 season. In April the club had nine league fixtures in addition to an Ayrshire Cup tie which doubled up as a testimonial for Sam McMillan. Midweek fixtures on the traditional Wednesday could not clear the backlog. Two Mondays had also to be utilised. The penultimate league fixture comprised a 4-0 win away to Stenhousemuir on a Monday evening. On the strength of that victory the Second Division title was won. It was now just a matter of calling on the remaining reserves of energy to conclude the league programme at home to East Fife two nights later. On the question of selection problems it could have been argued that the game was meaningless. Admittedly the league had already been won but the game was far from meaningless. A good crowd was expected to greet the champions and the Provost was an invited guest. Coach Ally MacLeod rather than manager Tom McCreath was the major influence in team matters. On taking stock Alex McAnespie and Ian Hawkshaw were still under suspension. Eddie Monan and Johnny Grant were both ruled out by injuries sustained against Stenhousemuir. John Cummings had scored twice in the title clinching match but he was not risked against East Fife. Eddie Moore did not score at Ochilview but nonetheless he was a most predatory striker. Yet he was pulled back to a half-back role for the Wednesday match. The solution taken was to recall John Balfour to the main striking role and to pair him with John Pullar.

On a beautiful sunny evening the crowd saw a team group photo being taken before the kick-off but one player was quite simply not recognised. John Pullar was a Junior trialist whose registered club was Petershill. In 1960s football Junior trialists were relatively common at Second Division level in Scotland. The distinction here was the occasion. This was his one and only game for the club yet he was photographed as part of the league winning squad. Captain Sam McMillan then introduced the players to Provost O'Halloran.

Davy Paterson (36) and John Balfour (76) scored in a 2-0 win. It was a nice send-off for Davy Paterson. He was on the list of free transfers so this was his last game. He signed for Berwick Rangers then made his debut against Ayr United in a League Cup tie at the start of the following season.

A human tide engulfed the field at the end. The players later appeared in the directors' box to acclaim the happy crowd and a roar went up that reached a crescendo. John Pullar had what was described as "a very promising debut." Mention of a debut would imply that he played again. He didn't but he must have departed with a very favourable impression of senior football. Was it like this all the time? If only! In season 1970/71 he made five league appearances for Queen of the South prior to which he had been registered with Hibs without making a first team appearance.

Ayr United 2 East Fife 0. Second Division.

Team: Millar, Malone, Murphy, Oliphant, Thomson, Moore, Davy Paterson, Pullar, Balfour, McMillan and Arthur Paterson.

Scorers: Davy Paterson, John Balfour.

The Ayr United forward line on 27th April, 1966.
Left to right: Davy Paterson, John Pullar, John Balfour, Sam McMillan and Arthur Paterson.

THE EPIDEMIC

Berwick Rangers versus Ayr United – 13th August, 1966

The year 2020 saw football played in extraordinary conditions. The global pandemic meant that when football did return the conditions were most stringent. In Scotland the Premier League was possessed of enough resources to resume on 1st August but necessity number one was that no supporters were admitted. Then we had the sight of coaching staff and substitutes socially distanced and wearing masks. Five substitutes being allowed was a further means of adapting. When the Scottish game was halted the first casualties were Queen of the South versus Ayr United and Motherwell versus Aberdeen, both scheduled for the Friday evening of 13th March. In the spirit of extreme optimism we were told that there would be no football for at least three weeks. The leagues became frozen with the positions in March being deemed the final positions. Eventually the Scottish Championship was scheduled to resume on 17th October with a programme of thirty-six matches narrowed down to twenty-seven.

Although nowhere near as extreme it was not the first time Ayr United had been in the midst of an epidemic. History has largely forgotten the Northumberland epidemic of foot and mouth disease which continued through July, August and September 1966. Ayr United's opening match of season 1966/67 was a League Cup sectional tie at Berwick. Contrary to logic Berwick is not situated in Berwickshire but in Northumberland which, at the time, was foot and mouth territory. Such epidemics are potentially fatal to farm animals. Infection within humans is rare but not impossible. At the time of this match there were travel restrictions from and to the infected areas and this did affect the gate for Ayr United's visit. The *Evening Times* report began: "Torrential rain and the foot and mouth restrictions hit the gate and a sparse crowd saw the first chance of the game fall to Ian Patterson, signed by Berwick from Ayr in the close season." The reporter managed to get both the Christian

Sam McMillan in his coaching years.

name and surname wrong. This was Davy Paterson. How sparse was the crowd? The reported figure was "fewer than 1,000". Before kick-off the teams were introduced to the Mayor of Berwick. His presence was a clear attempt to indicate that everything was normal. The heavy rain was bad news for the district since foot and mouth is a sneaky virus that is capable of being spread by precipitation.

Ayr United, newly promoted to the First Division, were expected to win this match. In line with that expectation the lead was taken in the 12th minute when Ian Hawkshaw slammed home a Johnny Grant cross. Bobby Bryce equalised in the 27th minute, his shot entering the net via a post. This was the first day on which Scottish teams could name a substitute. Ayr United's 'twelfth man' was Stan Quinn but he was not called upon. It finished 1-1. The other teams in the group were Raith Rovers and Cowdenbeath. With merely two wins out of six we contrived to win the group on goal average before going down to Rangers in the two-legged quarter-final.

Co-incidentally we were also in the same League Cup section as Berwick Rangers a year later. This time the Mayor did not appear but neither did the dreaded epidemic.

Berwick Rangers 1 Ayr United 1. League Cup.

Team: Millar, Malone, Murphy, Oliphant, Monan, Thomson, Grant, McMillan, Ingram, Hawkshaw and Paterson; substitute – Quinn.

Scorer: Ian Hawkshaw.

THE TEAM WITH NO NUMBERS

Ayr United versus Dunfermline Athletic – 29th August, 1970

There used to be a trick football question in circulation. The question was about who wore the number nine shirt for Celtic when they won the European Cup. Anyone falling for this was then appraised of the fact that no one wore a number nine shirt because Celtic's numbers were on their shorts. You will now be told about a team with no numbers on their shirts, shorts nor anywhere else.

For nearly four decades the Ayr United shirts had no numbers. Then, in October 1947, a rumour circulated that the club would soon be adopting numbers. These rumours were accurate. The numbers 2 – 11 indicated the position of the player. Only those flash continental goalkeepers had a number one on their back. The full evolution now allows us to see players being allocated a squad number which can be as high as 99. Putting the names of the players is another modern development. This is most beneficial to barrackers. In days of old a typical outburst from the Somerset Road end was: "Ye're an animal number nine." Nowadays the victim will have his name appended to the outburst rather than just his shirt number.

In the belief that shirt numbers were now mandatory it came as a surprise when Ayr United trooped onto the pitch for this First Division match in 1970 and the kit was totally devoid of numbers. The shirts were sky blue with no frills and the shorts were black. Ian Whitehead shot Ayr United ahead after just four minutes. Not that he needed a number for identification. His long hair and bustling style were more than apparent to the home fans. Having scored four minutes after the start he scored again with four minutes of the first half left. Then, in the final minute of the half, he headed his hat-trick. 3-0 to Ayr at the break and Whitehead could do no wrong. George McLean scored for Dunfermline in the 56th minute. Being in a Dunfermline shirt he was possessed of a shirt number but in his case too it was academic. He was instantly recognisable as one

Ian Whitehead

of Scottish football's great characters and he was less than three months away from becoming an Ayr United player. Seven minutes later Jacky Ferguson nailed it at 4-1 when he met a cross from John Doyle and dispatched it into the net with no need for a second touch. That evening we had the distinction of being Scotland's top-placed club. Motherwell too had won 4-1 so the honour was claimed merely on alphabetical order.

It took close to a half-century for another Ayr United player to hit a hat-trick in an opening league game. That player was Craig Moore and it happened in a 5-1 away win against Albion Rovers on 5th August, 2017. Yes, he did have a shirt number. It was number nine!

If you are looking for another of those trick football questions then try this one. Who wore the number nine shirt for Ayr United in the opening league game of season 1970/71?

Ayr United 4 Dunfermline Athletic 1. First Division.

Team: Stewart, Malone, Murphy, Fleming, Quinn, Walker, Young, Ferguson, Whitehead, Reynolds and Doyle; substitute – Hood.

Scorers: Ian Whitehead 3, Jacky Ferguson.

HAULED OVER THE WALL

Ayr United versus Kilmarnock – 12th September, 1970

Despite it being just the second Saturday of September this was the third Ayrshire derby of the season since the clubs had been drawn together in the same League Cup section. The first of those matches was at Rugby Park on the season's opening day. It was lost 1-0 to a Ross Mathie goal in the last minute. Ross Mathie – remember that name! He is the central character in this story. The return League Cup tie at Ayr took place a fortnight later and it was scoreless. It was immaterial since the section was won by Dundee. The other team in the section was St. Mirren.

With a distinct feeling of déjà vu Kilmarnock were back at Ayr on 12th September. Two points were at stake but an even bigger prize would be getting the better of our county neighbours. These League Cup matches had allowed a certain familiarity to grow. Familiarity is a diplomatic word for needle. When teams play each other several times in close proximity it is normal for personal feuds to develop between players. This in turn can lead to more competitive games. For the supporters it is different. On both sides of the Ayrshire divide these derbies are viewed with a degree of hostility regardless of the frequency.

Jim McSherry would go on to make a favourable impact for Ayr United at Premier League level but in this particular match he made his first team debut for Kilmarnock at the age of eighteen. Ally Hunter was outstanding in goal for the visitors but he was beaten in the 23rd minute. A Cutty Young cross was met by John Doyle who scored with a header. John Murphy continued to contain the threat of Tommy McLean but only for so long. In the final minute of the first half McLean managed to burst through to equalise.

It remained intensely fought but neither team succeeded in breaking the stalemate. On another day it could have been described as time being played out on a 1-1 draw. However it was not like that. In the closing minutes an incident occurred the like of which

SOMERSET NEWS

1/-
5p

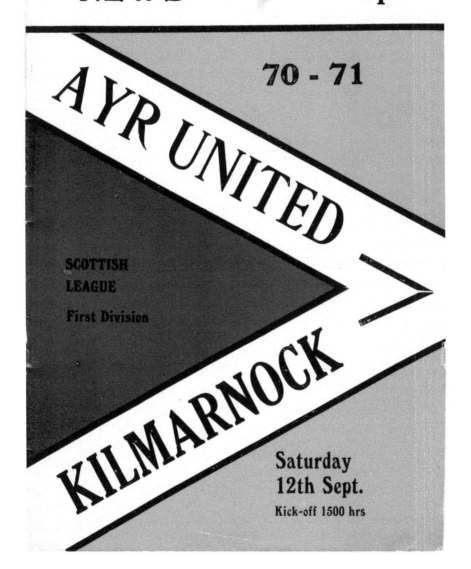

70 - 71

AYR UNITED

SCOTTISH
LEAGUE

First Division

KILMARNOCK

Saturday
12th Sept.
Kick-off 1500 hrs

had never happened before at Somerset Park and it has certainly not happened since. Ross Mathie was now on for Eddie Morrison and he went to take a throw-in on the far side roughly in line with the eighteen-yard line at the Railway End. He stepped back with the clear intention of getting the ball into the danger area and the next development was that he went backwards over the wall. Your writer viewed this incident from the Somerset Road end which was a distant vantage point. From personal recollection it looked as if he had simply stepped back too far whereupon he fell over the wall through his own momentum. Even from a distance it was curious to see a player on the terracing side of the wall with his boots in the air. Supporters, players, police and officials rushed to his aid. The player recovered to take the throw-in which was mercifully fruitless.

Although witnessing the incident I left the ground under the impression that Ross Mathie had just lost his balance. I was too focussed on the game to notice that the police had afterwards led a man away. When Mathie had stepped back to take the throw he was actually pulled over the wall by an Ayr United supporter. Nowadays an Ayr United supporter would not be in that section of the ground but in 1970 people could stand where they wanted. The first game at Somerset Park after segregation was introduced was against Hibs on 28th March, 1981.

In October 2004 Ayr United signed Graeme Mathie, the son of Ross Mathie. Did he get some fatherly advice to avoid Somerset Park? Probably not. Ross Mathie was a decent chap and we can reasonably guess that he had a forgiving nature.

Ayr United 1 Kilmarnock 1. First Division.

Team: Stewart, Malone, Murphy, Fleming, Quinn, Walker, Young, Ferguson, Whitehead, Reynolds and Doyle; substitute – Hood.

Scorer: John Doyle.

Visiting Player

ROSS MATHIE

Centre-forward — 5 ft 10 in., 11 st. 2 lbs.

Signed from Cambuslang Rangers in 1968, Ross quickly became a first team regular. He has the knack for being in the right place at the right time, and is especially dangerous in the air. This means trouble for defences whenever Tommy McLean sends over his accurate crosses.

Ross Mathie's feature in the programme on the day of the incident.

THE DOZEN

Ayr United reserves versus Cowdenbeath reserves –
12th December, 1970

When compiling football records the preoccupation is with matches falling into the definition of competitive. In this context competitive is not alluding to matches which have been closely fought. For record purposes the opposite is often true. Competitive is meant as falling under the auspices of league football or cups that have some status attached to them. Taking all matches into account Ayr United's highest win is 14-0 in the French-Canadian town of Saint Pierre. The match was so inconsequential that the result was barely noticed at the time. In denigrating the importance of minor matches it may seem a contradiction to record an account of a reserve match. The difference here is that this was a match which those in attendance did not forget. Eleven goals got scored in the second half, all but one of which came from the home team.

At this time reserve fixtures were a mirror image of the first team fixtures. The first team had a First Division match at Cowdenbeath while their counterparts at reserve level had a Reserve League match at Ayr. It was the second last weekend before Christmas and Ayr United still sought the first away league win of the season. These factors combined to explain why many did not sacrifice the time and expense to head to Fife.

The attendance at Somerset Park was sparse. Cowdenbeath reserves did nothing to fire the imagination of the public. Your writer attended most Ayr United away games in season 1970/71 but not the one on this day. It was a great pleasure to be one of the number at this Reserve League game and to experience the unanticipated euphoria. It took until the midway point of the first half for Ian Hume to open the scoring. In the 34th minute York scored for the visitors. This was a cold day and there was little happening out on the field to detract from just how raw it was. It took only four minutes for Ian Hume to re-establish the lead at 2-1 but the fans cared more for the approaching

Ayr United FC 1970/71.
Rear left to right: Alex McAnespie, George McLean, Jim Gilmour, Jim McFadzean, Davy Stewart, Rikki Fleming and John Murphy.
Seated left to right: Tommy Reynolds, Dougie Mitchell, Phil McGovern, Stan Quinn, Cutty Young, Davy McCulloch and John Doyle.

half-time when the PA system would relay news of how the big team was doing. Cowdenbeath 0 Ayr United 1 – the announcement was cheered. This was far more important than Ayr United reserves 2 Cowdenbeath reserves 1 at the corresponding stage. However what was about to happen at Somerset Park would make people forget that the first team match was even in progress. Two minutes after the break Alex McGregor scored. Then Jim Flynn, Alex McGregor again, Jim Flynn again and Neil Hood took it to 7-1 by the 62nd minute. Brian Lannon was sent on for Neil Hood and he took it to 8-1 just after appearing on the field. The spectators were unanimous in thinking that it was possible to hit double figures. Roger Sugden disturbed the momentum when he trimmed the substantial deficit to 8-2 but this was only the midpoint of the second half. Billy McGann's goal was quickly revisited and a flurry of scoring took place. Alex McGregor (73) 9-2; Jimmy Kinsella (77) 10-2; Frank McAleer (88) 11-2; Jim Flynn (89) 12-2. Taking the second half as a separate entity it was 10-1.

There was still time for the cherry on the proverbial cake. The tannoy appraised the public of the result from Central Park. At this time the announcer would let the fans know of an impending announcement by saying "Your attention please. Your attention please." Yes, he actually did say it twice. After getting the double attention of the drifting fans we got the happy news. "The result from Cowdenbeath is Cowdenbeath 1 Ayr United 3." It was the cue for another cheer.

Ayr United were strong at reserve level. In the following season the club went on to win the Scottish Reserve League.

Ayr United reserves 12 Cowdenbeath reserves 2. Reserve League.

Team: Gilmour, Wells, Filippi, McAleer, McAnespie, McCulloch, Kinsella, Flynn, Hood (Lannon), McGregor and Hume.

Scorers: Ian Hume 2, Alex McGregor 3, Jim Flynn 3, Neil Hood, Brian Lannon, Jimmy Kinsella, Frank McAleer.

Reserve League champions 1971/72. A home-made shield.

THE HOME GAME AT RUGBY PARK

Ayr United versus Rangers – 30ᵗʰ August, 1972

With season 1972/73 approaching it was already known that Somerset Park's returfing operation would not be finished on time. The opening fixtures were League Cup sectional ties against St. Mirren, Clydebank and Rangers. St. Mirren were beaten 2-1 at Dam Park in the opener. Eleven days later we retraced our steps to Dam Park having by then lost 1-0 at Clydebank then 2-1 in highly contentious circumstances away to Rangers. The defeat at Kilbowie Park was more than atoned for. On the banks of the River Ayr Clydebank were slain 5-0. Patients could be seen watching this game from the nearby County Hospital. The next sectional match was won 3-0 away to St. Mirren then came game six, against Rangers. Dam Park was clearly unsuitable when considered against crowd demands. Kilmarnock obligingly agreed that Rugby Park could host Ayr United's 'home' game. Although perhaps unaware of it they owed us this favour. Kilmarnock had twice played 'home' games at Somerset Park. On 15ᵗʰ April, 1916, they beat Hearts 3-1 in a First Division match at Ayr. Rugby Park was unavailable due to Cattle Show purposes. The next occasion was on 26ᵗʰ January, 1946, when they beat Partick Thistle 2-1 in what was then styled 'A' Division. At that time the reason for the switch to Ayr was "the present state of Rugby Park."

In later years our match against Rangers at Kilmarnock was sometimes misconceived as having been all-ticket. The misconception was caused by season ticket holders being issued with tickets. Ally MacLeod had a pre-match warning: "Rangers better not do too much experimenting. We are after them for this section. If we beat them by a minimum of 1-0 we share the top place. That would be a boost for our side."

On the night we went a goal down when Willie Johnston scored in the 26ᵗʰ minute. It was level in the 64ᵗʰ minute when Johnny Graham beat Peter McCloy with a clinical shot from outside the box. Derek

Ayr United 1972/73.
Rear left to right: Bobby Tait, Davy Wells, Jim Jackson, Alex McAnespie, Davy Stewart, Jim McFadzean, Rikki Fleming, George McLean and Jim Flynn.
Middle left to right: Willie Wallace (trainer), Brian Lannon, Stan Quinn, Ian Campbell, Joe Filippi, Ally McLean, Alex McGregor, Jim Grier, John Murphy, Phil McGovern and Willie McCulloch (assistant trainer).
Front left to right: Davy Robertson, Bobby Rough, John Doyle, Dougie Mitchell, Sam McMillan (coach), Alex Ingram, Ally MacLeod (manager), Johnny Graham, Hugh Thompson, Tommy Reynolds and Davy McCulloch.

111

Johnstone scored at the other end in an attack initiated from the recentre and there was no comeback. It was a 2-1 defeat. Rangers won the section but there was a new ruling which allowed runners-up to go through also so Ayr United progressed anyway.

That was on the Wednesday and the opening league game was at home to Rangers on the Saturday. There would be no immediate return to Rugby Park. It would take place at the beautifully returfed Somerset Park. Rangers had a high profile at this time. On 24th May they had won the European Cup Winners' Cup and their support was traditionally vast. Ally MacLeod cared nothing for reputations. The League Cup sectional ties between the clubs had created a lot of friction and they were about to clash again for the third time in a fortnight. There was gloom when Willie Johnston deposited the ball past Ally McLean in the fourth minute. Merely four minutes later John Doyle fired Ayr level. Nine minutes before half-time Alex Ingram scored with one of his trademark headers. It remained 2-1 and the sought after revenge was complete. One week later there was a return to Rugby Park but now the away dressing room and dugout got occupied. 1-0 to Ayr United this time and again it was an Alex Ingram winner, this time with his feet.

Ayr United 1 Rangers 2. League Cup sectional tie.

Team: McLean, Filippi, Murphy, McAnespie, Quinn, Fleming, Doyle, Graham, Ingram, McGovern and Stevenson; substitute – McCulloch.

Scorer: Johnny Graham.

THE MILK ROUND AND THE WORLD CHAMPIONS

Ayr United versus Dumbarton – 16th September, 1978

Some stories really could not be made up. Hugh Sproat's milk round could have cost the world champions the services of their manager. Although in the Premier League just months earlier Ayr United were part time. Having jobs outside of football can have drawbacks. For example in 1972 we played a Texaco Cup tie at Newcastle minus the services of Jim McFadzean who was a gym teacher at Loudoun Academy and he was denied the time off. On the Saturday before Christmas in 1986 Ayr United had a match against Meadowbank Thistle in Edinburgh and the team bus was delayed while postman Kenny Wilson finished his round. Maybe it was down to the increased exercise but he scored in a 2-2 draw. Nonetheless the vagaries of part time football could not be denied. In 1978 Hugh Sproat's nickname in the dressing room was Ernie. This was because he was employed as a milkman. If you are too young to understand the connection you may be told that there was a song about Ernie the fastest milkman in the west.

On the morning of the match with Dumbarton Mr Sproat wrenched his back while lifting a crate of milk bottles. The back-up goalkeeper was Richard Northcote who had already been told that, owing to a shoulder injury, he would not be playing in the corresponding reserve fixture at Dumbarton but it was considered that he had the lesser of the two injuries so he was selected for his league debut. The only first team game he had played in so far was a pre-season friendly away to Boston United the month before. Too severely injured to play for the reserves but thrust into league action – what could possibly go wrong?

There was extreme pressure to beat Dumbarton. After dropping out of the Premier League there was a virtual assumption that Ayr United would bounce back immediately but the opening weeks of the league season were sobering. After five matches we had one win, one draw

Hugh Sproat

and three defeats. This plunged the club to just above the relegation zone. In the midweek prior to the Dumbarton game Hamilton Accies had won 2-1 at Ayr. It was a match played out to choruses of "what a load of rubbish." Alex Stuart had even to deal with a player revolt. Billy McColl had played the entire ninety minutes against Hamilton but he complained about being listed as a substitute on the Saturday. He was punished for his protest by getting dropped from the squad. Danny Masterton replaced him as a substitute.

Contrary to the prevailing pessimism Ayr United contrived to play well. For a time! In the final minute of the first half Steve McLelland netted a header from a Gerry Christie cross. Three minutes beyond the break a Gordon Cramond shot struck a post and Gerry Phillips followed up to hit the rebound beyond the stricken Laurie Williams. At 2-0 this was enough to silence the doubters albeit that pre-match doubts were justified. The harmony was about to be most spectacularly disturbed. Murdo MacLeod (51), Derek Whiteford (52, 65), Jim Muir (71) and Derek Whiteford again (76) took it to Ayr United 2 Dumbarton 5. Five goals in twenty-five minutes – a small mercy was that the damage ended there. During that goal deluge it was clear that Richard Northcote's shoulder was giving him difficulty.

The defeat created even more public ire. Alex Stuart resigned although chairman Myles Callaghan stated that the board had exerted no pressure on him to quit. On the following Saturday an Ayr United team without a manager beat Clyde 1-0 at Shawfield. There was speculation that Ally MacLeod would soon be returning as manager. On the face of it this seemed like wild optimism because it would mean Mr MacLeod quitting his managerial role with the national team. However he did agree to talk to the Ayr United board. There was great delight locally when the announcement was made that he had agreed to return.

Jock Stein then quit his job at Leeds United to fill the Scotland vacancy. The consequence was speculation about who would be the next manager at Leeds. One of the names amidst this speculation was Cesar Luis Menotti who, at the time, was the manager of world champions Argentina. Menotti did not take up the appointment but let us recap on the whole chain of events.

Hugh Sproat wrenched his back on his milk round. The injured Richard Northcote played against Dumbarton and, through no fault of his own, had a bad game. Public ire was already simmering and the Dumbarton defeat saw it stoked up to such an extent that Alex Stuart resigned. Ally MacLeod's return to Ayr United then resulted in the national vacancy being filled by Jock Stein and subsequent talk about Cesar Luis Menotti taking on the Leeds job.

If Menotti had gone to Leeds it would have meant the world champions losing their manager due to Hugh Sproat injuring his back lifting a milk crate.

Ayr United 2 Dumbarton 5. First Division.

Team: Northcote, Wells, Connor, Hyslop, McAllister, Kelly, Phillips, Hannah, McLelland, Cramond and Christie; substitutes – Masterton and McLaughlin.

Scorers: Steve McLelland, Gerry Phillips.

VILHELM McCOLL

Rangers versus Ayr United – 3rd March, 1979

The importance of tactics cannot be understated. Robert Burns famously told us about what can go wrong with the best laid plans and his observation is all too apparent in football. What if the opposition do not play in the way that they are expected to? In an ideal world we would know definitively how the opposition intended to play. Surely this is a fanciful notion. Well a condition of this Ibrox friendly was that Ayr United would comply with the request from Rangers to play in the style of Cologne. This story is unique in football history. When else has a team had their tactics instructed by the opposition? In particular their boss John Greig wanted Ayr to play with two raiding wingers.

The match was on a Saturday. It was Scottish Cup day and Ayr United had already been eliminated at Aberdeen. Rangers would go on and win that season's Scottish Cup but they were left with a blank Saturday due to fixture chaos resulting in rescheduling. They were due to play in Cologne on the Tuesday in the first leg of a European Cup quarter-final. Asking Ayr United to play in the anticipated style of their opponents was deemed to be good preparation. Could Hugh (Hugo) Sproat mimic Harald Schumacher? Could Ian (Jan) McAllister do the same job in central defence as Bernd Schuster? Could Billy (Vilhelm) McColl be the same type of midfield general as Heinz Flohe? Could Gerry (Gerd) Phillips show the striking capability of Dieter Muller? Could the champions of Ayrshire remotely replicate the style of the champions of Germany? These are the questions. Here are the answers.

In the first half Ayr United's territorial domination was assisted by wind advantage. Yet the first goal was scored by Billy McColl three minutes after half-time. Scoring against the wind was in contradiction to what happened in the remainder of the game. Bobby Russell, Sandy Jardine (2), Gordon Smith and the wind carried Rangers to a 4-1 victory. The Ayr United cause would have been better served if Willie McLean had been allowed to dictate his own strategy. In the midweek prior Clyde had been beaten 5-0 at Shawfield and on the Saturday prior Montrose had been beaten 5-0 at Ayr. Ten First Division goals had been scored in the space of four days with none conceded.

Rangers lost 1-0 in Cologne to a Dieter Muller goal. The Scottish press considered that they were as good as in the semi-finals but they went out 2-1 on aggregate. Our first match after discarding the Cologne style was a midweek league fixture at home to Kilmarnock. Davy Wells headed an 87th minute winner.

There was an historical precedent for Ayr United playing a friendly at Ibrox. It had happened on 17th February, 1923, and on that day too there was a hint of the unusual about the background to it. It was the date of a scheduled league fixture between the clubs but Rangers had four players at Newcastle with the Scottish League squad. The decision was therefore made to substitute the league fixture with a friendly. In a 1-0 defeat the scorer was Carl Hansen who, as the name would suggest, was Danish. Foreign players were an extreme rarity in the Scottish game in that era.

Rangers 4 Ayr United 1. Friendly.

Team: Sproat, Wells, Kelly, Fleeting, McAllister, McColl, McSherry, McLaughlin, Phillips, Cramond and Connor; substitutes (all used) – Hannah, Scott, Masterton and Hendry.

Scorer: Billy McColl

Billy McColl

Gerry Phillips

Davy Wells

Robert Connor

WHAT'S HAPPENING? NO IDEA!

Dumbarton versus Ayr United – 26th January, 1980

This was a third round Scottish Cup tie and the Ayr support was substantial in the 2,480 crowd. Those of us who were there will not forget that afternoon. The fine detail of what happened is an altogether different matter. Failure to recollect the detail is not due to failings of the memory. It is due to a failure to view the action in the first place. The expression pea-souper is the clichéd description of a dense fog. You have to believe that this cliché is the most descriptive way to portray the mist enveloping Boghead Park while the cup tie action was allegedly taking place. Contemporary reports may or may not have been accurate. The precincts of the press area would not have afforded a clearer view. Not that any of us could argue with the printed accounts. From the terraces it was like trying to watch a football match through a bowl of milk.

With no pretence at accuracy here is an account of what is thought to have happened. In the 14th minute (the time is definitely accurate) Davy Armour struck a free-kick. It hit the Dumbarton wall then ricocheted beyond the stricken Laurie Williams to make it 1-0 to Ayr. There were conflicting reports about the scorer. Some credited Davy Armour and others marked it down as a Tommy Coyle own goal. If ever there was a day for muddled reports this was it. In the dying embers of the first half the bulk of the Ayr support started to trek towards the end the team would be shooting towards in the second half. While this ritual was underway Dumbarton equalised. Graeme Sharp was on the threshold of a fabulous career with Everton and Scotland. Here in 1980 he released the unmarked Brian Gallagher who equalised with the easy chance afforded to him.

At half-time a talking point was whether there was sufficient visibility for the game to continue. The lack of an abandonment was an act of optimism that the fog would clear. It didn't! In the 60th minute a Davy Armour cross was met by the raised hands of defender Ally MacLeod. Although the offence was barely visible to many it was

Ally Love

Davy Armour (not in the photo) scoring through the fog

Robert Connor's penalty winner – not visible to all.

a penalty nonetheless. Robert Connor thrashed the spot kick into the net and this was the winner. It gave rise to a nifty headline in the *Ayrshire Post*. Connor's nickname was Roger. The headline was ROGER AND OUT.

With the game won there was one further problem to contend with and it was a major concern. The fog had not lifted so the drive home was a slow and cautious one.

Dumbarton 1 Ayr United 2. Scottish Cup 3rd round.

Team: Rennie, McColl, Nicol, McSherry, McAllister, Fleeting, Frye, Armour, Morris, Connor and Christie; substitutes – Love and Hyslop.

Scorers: Davy Armour, Robert Connor.

Derek Frye (left) and Eric Morris (right) in the Boghead fog

THE ADVERTISING LOGO

Ayr United versus Hibs – 8ᵗʰ October, 1980

Shirt advertising is now expected. Much more of a rarity is the sight of a shirt without an advertising logo. The continentals were the innovators and it seemed an eccentric practice. It might even have seemed sacrilegious to desecrate a traditional shirt in this way. Now we can expect to see logos on sleeves, collars, shorts and socks. In this Wednesday evening match against Hibs an Ayr United team took to the field wearing an advertising logo for the first time. In the process it created a sensation of novelty. How odd that something now so familiar looked so strange. Yet there was professionalism to it. The historic logo bore the name of Barr Construction. History would be made on Hibs' next visit to Somerset Park too. This is a reference to the first game played here after the completion of the segregation fence (28ᵗʰ March, 1981).

The match in October was the first leg of a League Cup quarter-final. Eventually the focus of the 4,717 crowd was drawn towards the game rather than the shirts. In the 37ᵗʰ minute a Gerry Christie shot struck a post then fell perfectly for Derek Frye who beat Jim McArthur with a cool finish. Hibs then struck in the 43ʳᵈ minute when an Ally McLeod cross was met by the unmarked Terry Wilson who promptly scored. Eleven minutes beyond the break Stewart Rennie was beaten again when Ally McLeod headed home from a George Best corner-kick. George Best? Was this **THE** George Best? It actually was the legend himself. Thus far in the match Mark Shanks had been carrying out a man marking job on him. Parity was restored just three minutes later when a Gerry Christie corner-kick came over and Derek Frye managed to apply the finishing touch with a backheeler.

It remained 2-2 on the night. The result in the second leg was Hibs 0 Ayr United 2 after extra time. We were in the League Cup semi-finals for the third time to this point of the club's history, it only having happened previously in 1950 and 1969. What happened next?

Ayr United 1980/81. Back row left to right: Gordon Greenfield, Derek McCutcheon, Stevie Nicol, Kevin Hetherington, Ian McAllister, Robert Reilly and Laurie McGee. Middle row left to right: Willie McCulloch (assistant trainer), Mark Shanks, Billy McColl, David Armour, Billy Hendry, Derrick Hoy, Stewart Rennie, Alan McInally, Gerry Christie, Ian Cashmore, Eric Morris and Billy Smith (youth coach). Front row: Willie McLean (manager), Jim McSherry, Robert Connor, Jim Fleeting, Ally Love, Derek Frye and George Caldwell (assistant manager).

Supporters from that time will have little difficulty in remembering the 4-3 aggregate defeat against Dundee. Our next League Cup semi-final was in 2002 when an Eddie Annand goal was enough to reach the club's first major final. 2012 was the occasion of our next League Cup semi-final when there was a 1-0 defeat (after extra time) against Kilmarnock.

Football is apt to be rife with gimmickry but shirt advertising cannot be added to the list. It is a useful income source. Barr Construction remained loyal. Their logo remained on the shirts up to and including 1986/87. In turn the sponsors were then the *Ayr Advertiser*, Centrum, Arrow, Sports Division, What Everyone Wants, the *Ayrshire Post*, Barr Steel, Strachans, the *Ayrshire Leader*, Aurigin, Kerr & Smith, Kennedy Construction, GS Home Bakery, the Events Company, Rodie, Paligap, Bodog, Bitcoin BCH and Bitcoin SV.

Ayr United's first season was 1910/11. At that time there was one trackside advert at Somerset Park. It was on the far side and it was an advert for Fry's Cocoa.

Ayr United 2 Hibs 2. League Cup

Team: Rennie, Shanks, Nicol, McColl, Hendry, Fleeting, Frye, Love, Morris, Connor and Christie; substitutes – Larnach and McSherry.

Scorer: Derek Frye 2.

Jim Fleeting

THE DRUNKEN ANNOUNCER

Stirling Albion versus Ayr United – 1ˢᵗ January, 1981

Fixtures on New Year's Day used to be a joy. There would be a derby match and a bigger than average crowd. Thousands who attended were not regulars. Going to the football was the done thing on this day. It was permitted to carry in alcohol and the seasonal festivities would continue throughout the match. On a normal day a 'cairry-oot' would comprise a few cans or a half-bottle. At the New Year people were seen to enter the ground with hold-alls containing a large stash of drink. They even took in their own tumblers. At the start of 1981 there was no chance that watching Ayr United would be like the New Years of old. The derby match could not happen because Kilmarnock had managed to get into the Premier League in 1979. How about a semi-derby such as Morton? They were in the Premier League. St. Mirren? They were in the Premier League too. Queen of the South? They were a league below in the Second Division as were Stranraer. In the First Division Dumbarton were paired off with Clydebank and Hamilton Accies were paired off with Motherwell. It was inevitable that Ayr United would be ringing in 1981 against a club from the east. It was Stirling Albion away. That was a Thursday. Was there any hope of a tasty match on Saturday, 3ʳᵈ January? It was East Stirling at home.

From personal testimony you may be told that it was a mistake to arrive at Stirling much too early. A walk through the town was a bleak experience due to the obvious reason that it was New Year's Day and nowhere was open. Kick-off time was painfully slow in approaching and not even the picturesque setting of the Annfield ground did anything to lift the spirits. There was little point in even taking the time to ponder the prospects. This Ayr United team was in the promotion hunt albeit that Hibs and Raith Rovers were setting the pace. The home team was entrenched in the relegation zone and we had just beaten Dundee at home. Getting the points in the bag seemed like a formality. The operative word here is 'seemed'.

Then came the reading of the teams over the tannoy. Straight away it was apparent that the announcer was drunk. Not just tipsy but drunk! The team readings were heavily slurred. It was a mystery as to why Derek Frye was listed as a substitute rather than in the starting eleven but it is questionable whether anyone would have been able to discern this from the rambled rendition. By now most of us were convulsed in laughter.

At half-time it would have been sensible to allocate the PA duties to someone else unless, of course, the original announcer had sobered up. Well the microphone was not passed to someone else and neither was the incumbent any more sober. He was worse! The next home game was announced. It was a reserve game and he read the date as July instead of January.

During the second half he made random drunken announcements while play was still raging. In one of those announcements he named a Stirling Albion fan who wanted to wish the team the best of luck. At the time of that particular announcement your writer was standing a short distance away from two policemen who could not contain their mirth. They were clearly overcome by the infectious nature of the crowd laughter.

It had reached the stage where the game was a sideshow. In the entertainment stakes it came a poor second. Jim Fleeting scored but the home team levelled it through a Graeme Armstrong penalty. Eric Morris had a failed penalty attempt so it ended 1-1. We can be sure that the PA announcer was oblivious of the outcome.

Stirling Albion 1 Ayr United 1. First Division.

Team: Rennie, Shanks, Nicol, McColl, Hendry, Fleeting, Love, Armour, Morris, Connor and Christie; substitutes – Cashmore, Frye.

Scorer: Jim Fleeting.

Barr Construction became the shirt sponsor when the season was already in progress. The 1981/82 team group gave it its first airing in a squad photo.

THE NET MYSTERY

Ayr United versus Kilmarnock – 17ᵗʰ March, 1982

This was the rescheduling of the abandoned league fixture at Somerset Park on 4ᵗʰ January. On that day Kenny Hope decided that there would be no second half due to an unrelenting blizzard. When it was played on this March evening Motherwell had a commanding lead at the top of the First Division. The race for the second promotion place saw a tightly packed field comprising Hearts, Kilmarnock, Clydebank, St. Johnstone and Ayr United. Just three points separated the five contenders with Ayr United and Kilmarnock having the advantage of having played less games. Importance is attached to any Ayrshire derby but this one was vital. Again the official was Kenny Hope.

In the 26ᵗʰ minute Alan McInally struck the ball into the Killie net after it had been crossed by Eric Morris. The match then developed into a long stalemate in which neither side could break down the other. Yet if it could be maintained at 1-0 the home fans would go home in a chirpy mood. The closing minutes were understandably tense. Then, in the final minute, there were some confusing scenes surrounding a Kilmarnock equaliser. Derrick McDicken struck the ball from about thirty yards. Bob Shields' report in the *Evening Times* alluded to controversy: "Fans will probably debate until Doomsday the equaliser that Killie sensationally grabbed with barely a minute left to play."

Your writer witnessed the furore from the worst possible vantage point which was the extreme opposite end of the ground. After McDicken struck his shot it looked as if the ball had finished up on the track behind the Railway End goal. The testimony of the Ayr United defenders indicated that the ball clipped the outside of the post then struck a ball-boy and the boundary wall before entering the net from behind the goal. Some people thought that the ball did pass inside Stewart Rennie's right hand post but still finished on the track. Yet another opinion was that the ball had merely hit the

Ian McAllister.

David Armour.

Stewart Rennie.

Kevin Hetherington.

side netting. When Mr Hope indicated a goal he was surrounded by a deputation of protesting players. In fairness to him he agreed to consult a linesman but after a short confab the goal stood. Shortly afterwards the final whistle blew on a 1-1 draw and on the way off the beleaguered referee was continually protested to.

Kenny Hope was a fair and reasonable man. He even agreed to go back out and inspect the net. The four-man deputation was made up by manager Willie McLean, assistant manager George Caldwell and the linesman who had patrolled on the far side. It was a futile exercise. The goal was not going to be overturned.

On 1st February, 1997, a similar incident occurred at the Railway End. On that day we had a 1-0 victory in a top of the table six-pointer against Livingston. In first half stoppage time, with the game scoreless, Alain Horace headed the ball over Rab Douglas, the advancing goalkeeper. It looked as if defender Graham Watson managed to clear the ball off the line but, in the process, he ripped a hole in the net with his boot. It was claimed that the ball had crossed the line before being cleared through the hole in the net inadvertently created by the defender. There were no protests and the fans remained oblivious that anything out of the ordinary had occurred. Credence is added to the claim by the fact that this version of events was told by Livingston fans who had been standing behind that goal.

Ayr United 1 Kilmarnock 1. First Division.

Team: Rennie, Shanks, Ahern, Armour, McAllister, Hetherington, McInally, Ward, Morris, Connor and Christie; substitutes – Frye, Fleeting

Scorer: Alan McInally.

THE INJURED REFEREE

Ayr United versus Partick Thistle – 29th September, 1984

In 1984 Scottish football was suffering from alarming apathy. On the penultimate league Saturday of season 1983/84 the Kilmarnock versus Ayr United fixture attracted 1,495 to Rugby Park. In the previous month the teams had met at Ayr in the Ayrshire Cup final and for an Ayrshire derby the attendance of 883 was dire. Note that the word 'crowd' has been tactfully avoided. The game was far from being overpriced. When 1984/85 got underway the terracing price for adults at Somerset Park was £1.50. Even with due allowance for inflation this was a bargain. The opening league game drew 1,391 for a 1-1 draw at home to Hamilton Accies. One week later we were at Kilmarnock for a 0-0 draw played out in front of a miserly 2,013. It was a worrying level of disinterest for August. When Partick Thistle came to Ayr on 29th September the 2,222 gate was considered to be a good attendance. It helped that Partick Thistle fans have a liking for visiting Ayr. It is a convenient trip and it was a beautiful day. Home fans were attracted by an Ayr team unbeaten in the seven league games played to date although this statistic was tempered by five draws.

The game was only thirty seconds old when Ian McAllister brought down Alan Logan. Referee John Duncan immediately pointed to the penalty spot. He was instantly alerted by a flag waving linesman who pointed out that the offence had taken place outside the box. The resultant free-kick came to nothing. With seven minutes played an extraordinary chain of events got set in motion. A leg injury compelled the referee to limp off. His replacement was the senior linesman which was standard procedure. The contingency nowadays would be for the fourth official to take on the duties of the newly upgraded linesman. There was no fourth official. This was 1984! The refereeing supervisor then took over running the line. This was not an ordinary refereeing supervisor. It was Tom 'Tiny' Wharton, a legendary name in Scottish refereeing circles. He was now aged fifty-

Ayr United versus Partick Thistle, 19 25th September 1976

six. In 1992 he was awarded FIFA's Order of Merit. Never before had a former referee been bestowed with this honour. Wharton was quite simply an iconic figure. Here he was being coaxed out of retirement in 1984 and, quite naturally, he was immediately recognised by all except the younger fans. Alas the novelty lasted for no more than several minutes. Off-duty local referee Louis Thow took over.

The game itself was now looking like a sideshow. Yet it was a terrific match. The *Ayr Advertiser* report said that it "bristled with action and incident." In the 31st minute Gerry Collins scored with a header from a John McNiven cross. Gordon Dalziel, an Ayr United manager of the future, shot the equaliser ten minutes later. Jimmy Murphy then went on a mesmerising run before teeing up John McNiven to make it 2-1 to Ayr in time added on. Gerry Collins made it 3-1 with twenty minutes to go. Ten minutes later Ian Cochrane beat Hugh Sproat with a penalty that had been hotly disputed. It was very nearly 3-3 in the closing minutes when Hugh Sproat touched a goalbound shot onto a post.

It was a great match but nonetheless Tiny Wharton was the man who hogged the headlines. With eight matches now played the club sat in third place, beaten by Motherwell only on goal difference. Top-placed Airdrie had one point more and a handsome goal difference having just won 5-0 at Kilmarnock.

Ayr United 3 Partick Thistle 2. First Division.

Team: Sproat, Shanks, Buchanan, Morris, McAllister, Collins, Evans, McNiven, Sloan, Anderson and Murphy; substitutes – Irons, Adams.

Scorers: Gerry Collins 2, John McNiven.

For some the match developed into a sideshow.

THE FIRST PLASTIC PITCH

Stirling Albion versus Ayr United – 5th September, 1987

SECOND DIVISION
AYR PASS 'CARPET' TEST

Scotland's first competitive match on an artificial pitch took place at Stirling Albion's Annfield ground and the date coincided with a league visit from Ayr United. Artificial pitches are now commonplace but back in 1987 the idea seemed odd. The sense of novelty was so great that a crowd of 2,170 turned up. Our previous away game had been at Berwick a fortnight earlier and the gate was 524. Our next away game would be at Cowdenbeath a week later and the gate then was 484. The heading refers to a plastic pitch and it may look like a hint of criticism but that is how it was described by the media. It was a fair description anyway. The surface was not at all like the artificial surfaces of today. We now talk about pitches ranging from 2G to 6G. There are also hybrid surfaces and synthetic surfaces. In 1987 there was no such sophistication. Spectators at Stirling were left with the illusion of watching a match being contested on a hall floor. The ball was bouncing to unnatural heights and it wouldn't always stay in position in dead ball situations.

Opinions differed but the post match comments of the respective managers were positive. George Peebles offered this view: "Ayr were that bit quicker and looked more confident on the surface. This pitch will encourage speed and skill." Ally MacLeod succinctly stated: "The pitch suited my team." Ally was tactically shrewd and had given some thought to how the game should be approached. Ordinarily passing movements would require the ball to be passed in front of the player in order that he could catch it in his stride. The Ayr players were under instruction to pass the ball to the player's feet because, in Ally's words, "the ball was likely to run faster than on turf."

Jim Cowell

Who would be the first scorer on an artificial pitch in Scotland? Henry Templeton had the ball in the net in the first minute but he was denied his place in history when flagged for offside. In the 26th minute John Sludden got pulled down for a penalty. Tommy Walker then stepped up with a great chance of making history. He too was denied. Andy Graham saved the spot-kick. Brian Kemp scored the historic goal at the other end with a twelve-yard strike in the 37th minute. It was squared at 1-1 midway through the second half. Kenny Wilson had been on the field for only three minutes when he created panic in the Stirling defence then laid on a chance from which Henry Templeton scored. Templeton was the game's star player. He was so skilled that his natural footballing ability would have left him feeling at ease on virtually any surface.

With five league fixtures played, top place was occupied on goal difference. One week later a 6-1 romp at Cowdenbeath comprised the first of eight consecutive league wins. On 26th March, 1988, we were back at Stirling to play out a 2-2 draw which guaranteed promotion. Three weeks after that we decanted east once more to clinch the league title at Alloa.

Stirling Albion 1 Ayr United 1. Second Division.

Team: Watson, McIntyre, Hughes, Furphy, McAllister, Evans (Wilson 64), Templeton, Scott, Walker, Sludden and Cowell; unused substitute – McCracken.

Scorer: Henry Templeton.

After inaugurating the carpet our return to Stirling on 26th March, 1988, clinched promotion.

THE FITNESS TEST IN THE STREET

Meadowbank Thistle versus Ayr United – 20ᵗʰ August, 1988

In bygone days a broken down bus at the side of the road was far from an uncommon sight. By 1988 it was a somewhat rarer sight. We can put this down to progress. However this progress in the evolution of buses did not render them totally immune to mishaps such as the one that happened when the Ayr United squad travelled to Edinburgh to face Meadowbank Thistle. After a gloriously won promotion this was our second game back in the second tier. The opener had resulted in a 3-2 win at home to Clydebank.

When the Ayr United bus entered Edinburgh there was a definite confidence. With Ally MacLeod in charge it could have been no other way. Then the bus broke down. It happened in the Haymarket area. The problem was put right after a delay but Mr MacLeod put the hold-up to good use. There was a concern over Henry Templeton's fitness. Rather than wait until the Commonwealth Stadium was reached he ordered Henry out of the bus there and then to go through a fitness test. In the street! This could have been interpreted as a typical Ally MacLeod gimmick yet below the comic veneer there was a practical purpose. The sight of Henry doing sprints along the pavement caused bemusement to passers-by. When the story broke initially it was an even better tale. Something clearly got lost in translation. Media reports told of the bus breaking down in Princes Street and Henry Templeton weaving past shoppers during his fitness test. To shoppers we can add festival goers. What a story it was! The crux of it was true but the location was untrue. It definitely happened in the Haymarket area but even there it must have looked like a publicity stunt for a Fringe event. Street entertainment is, after all, an integral part of Edinburgh life at the time of the Fringe. Henry's fitness test was surely more entertaining than the stereotypical juggling, fire-eating, trick cycling or mime.

Meadowbank Thistle versus Ayr United was not an Edinburgh Festival event but it would surely have been more entertaining than some of the events. Tommy Walker put the team ahead in the 33rd minute from all of three yards. There was a panicky incident in the second half when a penalty was conceded. Meadowbank striker Des Walker proceeded to slam his spot-kick against the crossbar. It was costly for the home team. At the opposite end Henry Templeton made it 2-0 with a great drive. The judgement that he had been fit to play was now fully justified. John McGachie headed the ball beyond George Watson in the final minute but there was insufficient time to pose a threat to an Ayr win.

It is the custom to bestow awards to the best performers at the Fringe. Is it too late to retrospectively nominate Henry Templeton for the best street entertainer at the 1988 event?

Meadowbank Thistle 1 Ayr United 2. First Division.

Team: Watson, McIntyre, Love, Furphy, McAllister, Evans, Templeton, Wilson, Walker, Sludden and Cowell; substitutes – Ross, McCracken.

Scorers: Tommy Walker, Henry Templeton.

Henry Templeton going through a more conventional fitness test.

Ayr United FC 1988-89

Our return fixture with Meadowbank Thistle took place on 3rd December, 1988. Tommy Walker is in the act of scoring

THE DUG

Ayr United versus Morton – 1ˢᵗ March, 1994

The 'dug oan the park' used to be an occasional sight at Scottish football matches. A dog could easily squeeze underneath the turnstile then show equal agility by clambering over the wall. The large swathe of well-tended grass must have been like doggy heaven to those canine creatures who remained oblivious to the football match taking place. Traditionally the seagull is the creature more likely to visit Somerset Park. Seagull? Why the singular? In the early weeks of the football season entire flocks seem to inhabit the ground. As the season progresses their diminishing numbers has no correlation to the standard of football. It is more to do with the habits of seagulls. The behavioural habits of seagulls is a study outwith your writer's area of expertise but before departing this topic it is worth telling the tale of what happened on the evening of 25ᵗʰ July, 2007, when Motherwell were at Ayr for a friendly. Goalkeeper Mark McGeown found himself under more threat from the seagull attack than the Motherwell attack. At one stage what looked like a whole pack of them flew at him at the Somerset Road end. Fortunately it was an otherwise quiet phase of the game for him. He looked decidedly fazed. Barry John Corr replaced him at half-time. It is to be hoped that this was the plan all along rather than conceding to the aggression of the winged pests. Somerset Park is in the Hawkhill district of the town. You would be correct in assuming that the area used to be frequented by hawks. This leads to the conclusion that there would have been no seagulls causing a nuisance at the ground in the pioneering years.

Ayr United's second match after the war was at Alloa on 18ᵗʰ August, 1945. A rabbit appeared at Recreation Park that afternoon. It was reported that a spectator captured it. Captured – this implies that it ended up in someone's stewpot. These post war days were austere and rationing was still in force. A Clyde match at Shawfield once had to be held up because a swan appeared on the pitch. The visitors that day happened to be Hearts. There would be so much more joy in telling this tale if the visiting team had been Ayr United.

Ayr United FC 1993/94

Malky Shotton

It is now time to tell the story of 'the dug' in the heading. Morton were the visitors on the first night of March 1994, it having been postponed from the Saturday due to freezing conditions. Five teams were due to take the drop at the end of the season due to the impending reconstruction of the leagues. Seventh place had to be achieved for safety and we were dangerously close to the cut. Morton were second bottom. The chance to consolidate was taken although there were fears when Rowan Alexander headed past Willie Spence with fifteen minutes played. It was the 66th minute before the equaliser materialised. A shot from Brian Bilsland was parried by David Wylie into the path of Malky Shotton who fired it home. It was his third goal for Ayr United and each one was against Morton. Jim Tolmie got sent off for a second bookable offence with five minutes left. The numerical advantage was immediately exploited. Before Tolmie had even reached the bath water his team was behind. A Gordon Mair cross was badly cleared. This afforded Brian Bilsland to take the chance to unleash a ferocious drive into the net from eighteen yards. He celebrated wildly and so did the fans. The celebrations were starting to subdue when a greyhound ran onto the pitch. This was before the recentre had even taken place. Coaxing the dog off the pitch was difficult. It ran about aimlessly and it kept eluding its would-be captors. However it did not elude Malky Shotton who caught it and carried it off the field. Would you have backed this dog in a greyhound derby? Ponder this – Big Malky caught it! On the same evening a fox ran onto the field during a Celtic versus Kilmarnock game.

Six decades earlier greyhounds might have been regular visitors to Somerset Park. In May 1932 the Ayr United board declined an offer to use the ground for dog racing. A new dog track opened at Limekiln Road the following year.

Ayr United 2 Morton 1. First Division.

Team: Spence, Traynor, Mair, Shotton, Hood, Lennox, Biggart (Woods 70), Moore, McGivern, Jack (Bilsland 53) and McGlashan; unused substitute – Duncan.

Scorers: Malky Shotton, Brian Bilsland.

Brian Bilsland

THE GOALIE ON THE WING – EPISODE 4

Ayr United versus Berwick Rangers – 2nd March, 1996.

Precisely six months to the day earlier (2nd September 1995) Berwick Rangers had won 4-1 at Ayr amidst a welter of vocal disapproval. On the Tuesday after the match manager Simon Stainrod said that he would not be resigning. Less than three hours later his resignation was announced. When next visiting Somerset Park the chances of Berwick Rangers winning by any score at all were slim. This was despite Berwick being third in the league at the time and Ayr United being third bottom. The damage had been done in the first half of the season after which the slump was arrested by manager Gordon Dalziel's strenuous efforts at recruitment. In season 1995/96 the club used forty-five players in competitive action. At the time this was a club record. Two seasons later that turnover was exceeded by one to create what remains the club record for turnover. You will have correctly surmised that transfer windows did not exist then. For your writer the March 1996 match against Berwick Rangers was a statistical dream. The statistics arising from a 5-0 win were:

The first time an Ayr United team had scored five in a competitive fixture since a 5-3 home win over Dumbarton on 21st November, 1992.

The first hat-trick by an Ayr United player since Gordon Mair in the Dumbarton game just referred to.

The first win by at least a five-goal margin since beating Meadowbank Thistle 7-0 at home on 21st September, 1991.

The Meadowbank goalkeeper that day was the same Jim McQueen who was the Berwick goalkeeper in this match in March 1996.

Danny Diver became only the fifth player in the club's history to hit a debut hat-trick or better. The others were: Tom Newall – hat-trick in a 4-1 away win over Leith Athletic on 22nd February, 1913; Willie Fleming – hat-trick in a 5-0 home win over Arbroath on 22nd August, 1925; Jimmy Smith – hat-trick in a 4-4 draw at home to King's Park on 13th August, 1927; Andy Torrance – five in an 8-1 home win over Forfar Athletic on 28th March, 1953.

The attendance of 907 was the first three-figured attendance for a competitive game at Somerset Park since the 971 figure on 6th September, 1986, when Berwick Rangers were also the visitors. Here in 1996 the low attendance was partly blamed on televised rugby. It was Scotland versus England. A Scotland win would have secured the Grand Slam and the Calcutta Cup. It was a Scotland defeat.

There were yet more talking points arising from Berwick's demise. Finnish striker Tommi Paavola hit two debut goals. There was also the scintillating form of Paul Kinnaird who set up all five goals. Drama was also added to the mix. The following day's *Sunday Mail* carried a story stating that there had been a run of bets in the Edinburgh area for Ayr United to win 5-0.

We are all aware of the principle of saving the best for last. That principle will now be gloriously applied. The afternoon's major talking point was something else altogether. Those of us who were present are unlikely to forget this episode. If it was before your time it is to be hoped that you will take great delight in being appraised of this tale.

In the 82nd minute Gregg Hood picked up a knock and had to go off. It had been 4-0 at half-time and 5-0 since the 57th minute. Gordon Dalziel had gone on for Evan Balfour in the 60th minute and Kevin Biggart had gone on for Willie Jamieson in the 75th minute. The only remaining substitute was Kenny Barnstaple. So where was the problem? Barnstaple for Hood was surely a straightforward substitution, especially since there were no alternatives. Well there was the hint of a problem. Kenny Barnstaple was a goalkeeper! He was deployed on the right wing and almost straight away he was a ringing endorsement of the argument that goalkeepers are really frustrated outfielders. Every time the bold Kenny was in possession he was cheered and in what remained of the game he got more than his fair share of time on the ball. Rather than restricting his game to a simple pass to the nearest team mate he kept opting to attempt mazy runs. The reason he had so much possession was attributable to his extreme reluctance to part with the ball. He put his head down and went for glory. The fans just loved his display and it surpassed all else that had happened in the entire match.

Ayr United 5 Berwick Rangers 0. Second Division.

Team: Duncan, Napier, Connie, Hood (Barnstaple 82), Jamieson (Biggart 75), Sharples, Balfour (Dalziel 60), Diver, Paavola, Henderson and Kinnaird.

Scorers: Tommi Paavola 2, Danny Diver 3.

Robert Scott sporting the purple and green. The opponent is Jose Quitongo and the venue is Fir Park.

THE PURPLE AND GREEN

Dumbarton versus Ayr United – 5th October, 1996.

The premise of the Ayr United shirt is traditionally simple. In the main we can expect to see shirts which are predominantly white and shorts which are black. Inevitably there will be logos and embellishments. On a recurring basis we can even expect a return to black and white hoops. Black and white – these have been the club colours since the board decided to discard the original crimson and gold in 1914. War being declared weeks afterwards was merely coincidental! In the modern game it is dictated that clubs must now possess change shirts. These are worn not only when there is a colour clash. They are labelled 'away shirts' and are frequently worn to satisfy commercial interests. Designers have endless possibilities since they are not constrained by tradition. This can have the potential to induce the Marmite syndrome.

In early October 1996 Ayr United were going strong in the inappropriately named Second Division. It was the third tier! With seven games played it was developing into a three-club race for the title. The other clubs were Livingston and Hamilton Accies. These would remain the competing clubs until the season's end and many of you are sure to remember the title being won at Berwick. The attendance at Dumbarton was 939 which included a noisy visiting support. Boghead Park was one of those traditional Scottish football grounds, often maligned although sometimes unfairly. The ground name made it an easy target for cheap comment.

It is not common practice for fans to pay particularly close attention to players going through their pre-match routine but on that day at Dumbarton some of us were vigilant enough to notice that our players were wearing a combination of green and purple beneath the conventional training tops. It was only when the team took to the field that we could view the strip in all of its 'explosion in a paint factory' glory. This was revolutionary. No Ayr United team had ever before turned out in anything quite like this. The shirts were of green and purple halves, the shorts were also of green and purple halves and the socks were purple. Immediately the comments were either highly favourable or highly unfavourable. There was no middle ground. Would the unfavourable opinion be swayed if we performed well in it? For example you may recall a 5-0 defeat away to Queen of the South on 1st September, 2018. Get rid of the all-pink kit was the popular refrain. Four weeks later we had a 5-1 away win against Morton and that particular kit was viewed differently.

The purple and green also had a bad start. In the 13th minute Steve Dallas broke through and lobbed the ball over Henry Smith to make it 1-0 for Dumbarton. Minutes later Dallas found himself in the same situation and he again tried a lob. It cleared the crossbar but not by much. In the 28th minute Jim Mercer rounded goalkeeper Ian MacFarlane then cut the ball back for Paul Kinnaird to equalise with a header. Four minutes later Kinnaird was pulled down by Martin Melvin. Penalty! Paul Smith took it and MacFarlane pulled off a good save. In the 37th minute Paul Smith crossed for Darren Henderson to score with a header. It finished 3-1 with a goal in extraordinary circumstances. Ten minutes after the break Robert Connor's cross was turned towards goal by Isaac English. The ball slipped through the goalkeeper's hands. At the opposite end of the ground the Ayr support did not acclaim the goal because none of us realised that the ball had actually crossed the line. The realisation came when the players started filtering back for the re-centre. There were accusations of the team looking like court jesters. Why worry? The game was won.

Did the purple and green halves get consigned to history? No. In the summer of 2020 the club launched a change kit of the same design.

Dumbarton 1 Ayr United 3. Second Division.

Team: Henry Smith, Traynor, Watson (Biggart 82), Coyle (Law 40), Hood, Connor, Paul Smith, English, Mercer (Colin Smith 77), Henderson and Kinnaird. .

Scorers: Paul Kinnaird, Darren Henderson, Isaac English.

Paul Kinnaird sporting more conventional attire.

THE LAST GAME AT CAPPIELOW

Morton versus Ayr United – 1ˢᵗ May, 1999.

This was the last game at Cappielow before Morton started to ground share at Airdrie. Well, that was how the game was advertised. Even the commentator on Football First managed to get vaguely emotional when describing Cappielow's last match. Morton had played here since 1879. Moving away after 120 years seemed quite sensational, especially since Airdrie was forty miles down the M8. The emotional attachment to the ground was not reflected in the attendance. Normally 2,337 would have been a reasonable crowd for a relatively meaningless game at the tailend of the season. In the context of this being Cappielow's last game (or so we thought) it was disappointing. Almost ten years to the day earlier (29ᵗʰ April, 1989) Ayr United had met St. Johnstone in the last game played at Muirton Park. That ground did not have as deep a history as Cappielow. The opening match was on Christmas Day 1924. Nevertheless it was an old established ground. For its closing match the attendance was 6,728. The result was St. Johnstone 0 Ayr United 1, the scorer being former St. Johnstone player John Sludden. The hope was that Cappielow's farewell would also coincide with an Ayr United win. How did the home fans feel about Morton's move? Quite frankly they were bitter.

Gordon Dalziel was on a scouting mission at the Livingston versus Inverness Caledonian Thistle fixture therefore Iain Munro was in charge of team matters at Greenock. When the match got underway Munro's team was not unduly tested. With six minutes played Glynn Hurst headed a John Traynor cross beyond Ally Maxwell. In the 22ⁿᵈ minute Hurst's pace gave him the freedom to gain ground down the left flank before crossing to Andy Walker who had time to tee his shot up before scoring. Four minutes before half-time a mistimed punch by David Castilla allowed John Anderson a simple goal from a few yards. Three minutes later the ball was in the net at the other end after Andy Walker shot home a Gary Teale pass. By the 79ᵗʰ minute it was Morton 1 Ayr United 4. Glynn Hurst released John Davies who tried a lob which was insufficiently cleared and he scored with a header from the rebound.

The final whistle was the cue for an onfield demonstration. This had nothing to do with the performance and everything to do with the planned move to Airdrie. STV captured the scenes and there were interviews asking the fans how they felt about it. It was perfectly obvious how they felt about it but the question had to be asked.

Match reports had copious references to the curtain being drawn on Cappielow. Quite correctly this was a far bigger story than the actual match. If you drive along the A8 past Cappielow today you will see a football ground and not a housing estate or supermarket. Back in 1999 the move to Airdrie was publicised as a done deal. It was not a case of the media getting it wrong. The move really was on. Until a u-turn!

Ayr United's next visit to Cappielow was on 18th September, 1999. The 'home' team was Clydebank who were sharing the ground. Once more there was a demonstration. It came from Clydebank fans who were most vocal about the direction of their club. Completing Groundhog Day was an Ayr win (2-0).

Morton 1 Ayr United 4. First Division.

Team: Castilla, Traynor, Barrick, Millen, Campbell, Findlay, Hurst, Davies, Walker (Bradford 88), Teale (Bowman 80) and Lyons (Reynolds 66).

Scorers: Glynn Hurst, Andy Walker 2, John Davies.

Neil Tarrant (10) has just scored after twenty seconds.

BEGINNING MIDDLE AND END

Ayr United versus Morton – 5th February, 2000.

Clubs prefer the fans to arrive in good time before the kick-off. It minimises issues of stewarding and crowd safety. In a perfect world fans would adhere to punctuality. Of course we live in an imperfect world and it is to be expected that there will be latecomers. It can happen quite innocently such as when the brain tells you that there is still time for another quick pint. Regardless of the reasons you can be sure that the turnstiles are still clicking when the game is already in progress. Another trait is to miss the closing minutes of the first half in order to get a good place in the pie queue. For terracing dwellers at Somerset Park this presents few problems because the game is still visible while queuing at the various kiosks but the kiosks in the Stand are concealed from the on-field action. Let us now look at another trait. There are supporters who habitually leave a few minutes before the end. The reason is the obvious one of getting away ahead of the crowd. Rangers even have a label for such fans. They are called the subway loyal.

Let us put these traits together in order to imagine a fan who 1. Gets in a few minutes late. 2. Slips away to a kiosk two or three minutes before the half-time whistle. 3. Departs a few minutes before the end to avoid the traffic. If we apply this to 5th February, 2000, the fixture would have had the illusion of ending Ayr United 0 Morton 2. However Ayr United won the match with goals quite literally at the beginning, the middle and the end.

Straight from the kick-off Gary Teale was released and he set off on a run which saw him beat three defenders before crossing for Neil Tarrant to head the ball beyond Ally Maxwell for a goal timed at twenty seconds. This created a club record at the time. The previous record for the fastest goal had been held by Glynn Hurst who scored after twenty-two seconds at Motherwell on 18th August, 1998. On 29th July, 2017, Ross Docherty created the current club record with a goal after fifteen seconds at Annan.

Mickey Reynolds in action against Morton on 5th February, 2000.

As the Morton match progressed it became very intriguing. At the heart of the visitors' defence former Ayr United players Derek Anderson and Andy Millen were in a determined mood but equally determined was the Ayr United strikeforce comprising Neil Tarrant and Glynn Hurst. In the 38th minute Paul McDonald's deep cross allowed David Murie to steal in at the back post to equalise with a low shot. By dint of the spoiler in the preamble you will know that Ayr United scored next. In first half stoppage time John Anderson deliberately handled Glynn Hurst's netbound header on the line. The errant defender was sent off and Glynn Hurst netted the resultant penalty. Somerset Park's Railway End must have caused Mr Anderson nightmares. On Morton's previous visit (2nd October) Nigel Jemson was pulled down by Ally Maxwell who got sent off. John Anderson donned the goalkeeper's jersey but failed to stop Nigel Jemson's spot-kick which tied up a 3-0 win. In March 2004 I attended a Bristol Rovers versus York City match along with my son David. Before the match we were invited into the home dressing room to meet the players (incredible but true). One of those players was John Anderson who was on the point of making his Bristol Rovers debut. In conversation the topic of Somerset Park was diplomatically avoided.

Let us revert to the topic. In the 62nd minute Glynn Hurst pushed Paul McDonald for a Morton penalty. McDonald took it and Craig Nelson saved it only for Harry Curran to rifle home the rebound for 2-2. In stoppage time a Gary Teale corner-kick was met by Glynn Hurst who scored with a powerful header that entered the net via a post for a much celebrated winner.

The afternoon's events carried three lessons. Get in on time. Be careful about when you go for a pie. Do not slip away too early.

Ayr United 3 Morton 2. First Division.

Team: Nelson, Robertson, Rogers (McMillan 64), Shepherd, Craig, Duffy, Teale, Wilson, Hurst, Tarrant (Crilly 60) and Reynolds (Grant 60).

Scorers: Neil Tarrant, Glynn Hurst 2.

HAPPY HOLIDAYS AND
THANKS FOR YOUR SUPPORT
AYR UNITED SUPPORTERS CLUB

FOUR PENALTIES CONCEDED: TWO REFEREES: NINE MEN

Forfar Athletic versus Ayr United – 16ᵗʰ October, 2010.

The 2010/11 season is mainly remembered for the promotion winning scenes at Brechin. To the anoraks amongst us this particular campaign might also be remembered as a statistical dream.

> Nineteen penalties awarded. Mark Roberts scored fourteen and had two saved (both saved by Michael Brown of East Fife). Andy Rodgers scored two and Alan Trouten converted one.

> Sixteen penalties conceded of which fourteen were scored and two saved (by David Crawford in the one match).

> Nine red cards for Ayr United one of which was overturned.

> Ten red cards for the opposition.

> Two own goals in Ayr United's favour.

> Three own goals in the opposition's favour.

This was remarkable. Thirty-five penalties, nineteen red cards and five own goals. In a 3-2 win away to East Fife on 18ᵗʰ September, Mark Roberts became the only player ever to score a hat-trick of penalties for the club. Four weeks later, at Forfar, penalties again became the major talking point, albeit not favourably. For the first and only time in the club's history, four were conceded.

It all went wrong from the start or rather the delayed start. It kicked-off fifteen minutes late due to traffic chaos on the M90. Some of the Ayr support did not arrive until a while later. Match referee Craig Charleston did not make the start either. He too was caught up in the traffic. Assistant referee Colin Brown took charge for the first

David Crawford saving one of the four Forfar penalties. The taker was Ross Campbell. Note the advert behind the goal offering a cure for neck pain. For anyone involved with Ayr United this match was a definite pain in the neck.

half. Penalty number one to Forfar came in the 12th minute when Dean Keenan pulled down Scott Allan. Ross Campbell scored. It remained 1-0 until half-time. Craig Charleston then took over the refereeing duties. In the 59th minute Chris Templeman made it 2-0. Disappointing though it was, the home team's lead was merited. Ross Robertson went close to scoring with a strong header that was brilliantly saved. He was later shown a yellow card. Colin Brown then drew attention to the fact that he had yellow-carded Robertson in the first half so it was a sending-off. In the 75th minute Dean Keenan brought down Martyn Fotheringham for a second Forfar penalty. It was also deemed worthy of a second yellow card. This time David Crawford saved Ross Campbell's spot-kick. Eleven versus nine and two down at an advanced stage of the game, the situation looked impossible. Just one minute later we had Forfar penalty number three after a foul by William Easton. There was a switch of taker and Crawford saved Scott Allan's penalty too. Mr Charleston was possessed of enough willpower to let the game run for another five minutes before awarding Forfar their fourth penalty when Martyn Fotheringham went down in the box again. This time the supposed transgressor was Martyn Campbell. Could this be a hat-trick of penalty saves? It wasn't. Fotheringham scored for 3-0. William Easton slammed home an Andy Rodgers cross for 3-1 but shortly before the end Graham Gibson scored for Forfar. Quite remarkably their last goal was from open play.

Forfar Athletic 4 Ayr United 1. Second Division.

Team: Crawford, Tiffoney (Taggart 61), Easton, Malone, Campbell, Robertson, Trouten, Keenan, McKay (Reynolds 73), Roberts (Rodgers 73) and McLaughlin; unused substitutes – Smith and McWilliams.

Scorer: William Easton.

THE FOURTH SUBSTITUTE

Queen's Park versus Ayr United – 24th January, 2017

The concept of allowing substitutes was introduced to Scottish football in time for the start of season 1966/67 although the scheme was deferred to 1967/68 for the Scottish Cup. It is true that there are reports of Ayr United using substitutes in earlier years but only in friendlies. Even in friendlies the practice was highly infrequent. When the idea became reality for competitive football in this country just one substitute was permitted. This gave rise to the expression 'twelfth man'. Stan Quinn was the first Ayr United player to be used as a substitute in a competitive match. This happened on 20th August, 1966, when he replaced Dougie Mitchell in a League Cup tie at home to Cowdenbeath. Let us now explore the relevance of this topic in relation to 2017.

A fourth round Scottish Cup pairing with Queen's Park had ample historical precedent. The clubs had previously met in the competition in 1921, 1938, 1949, 1951, 1975, 1988 and 2013. Each time Ayr United had progressed with the exception of 1975. That solitary defeat was a real shock considering that the game was at Ayr and the team had a good representation of players who are now deemed to be club legends.

Merely 1,326 turnstile clicks registered at Somerset Park when Queen's Park were here for their 2017 cup visit. In 2013 it had been an even more miserly 879, this being blamed on the heavy rain. It was a clear indication that the allure of the Scottish Cup was fading. In 1938 the crowd was 17,204 when the clubs met here in a Wednesday afternoon replay. The comparatively depleted crowd of 2017 witnessed a scoreless draw. On the Tuesday evening the replay took place at a ghostly Hampden Park. 1,326 turned up. In 1951 the Hampden tie between the clubs had drawn 23,000. On that same afternoon in 1951 the attendance at nearby Ibrox was 102,342 for the Rangers versus Hibs tie. It was only the third round! Reverting from 1951 to 2017 you may be told that Ayr United faced the prospect of defeat. Paul Woods (4) – Queen's Park, Craig Moore (26) and Bryan Wharton (32) – Queen's Park had the home team 2-1 up, a scoreline persisting until dangerously late. Conrad Balatoni (83) headed a tie-saver. Seven minutes into extra time Queen's Park's Sean Burns got sent off after being shown a second yellow card yet it still proved difficult to break the deadlock.

In the first minute of time added on in extra time (120 + 1) the illuminated board was held up to signal an Ayr United substitution. This caused a stir. The fans were mindful that Paul Cairney had gone on for Brian Gilmour, Alan Forrest had gone on for Michael Donald and Craig McGuffie had gone on for Craig Moore. How could Michael Rose now go on for Nicky Devlin? It was common knowledge that only three substitutes could be used from the nominated seven. The common knowledge was misplaced. A new ruling had been brought in for the 2016/17 Scottish Cup whereby a fourth substitute was allowed in extra time. This was the first instance of this ruling being used. The whistle blew a matter of seconds later yet Michael Rose had made history as the fourth substitute. Ian McCall had obviously identified him as a key player in the impending shootout.

A tense shootout was won 5-4, Greg Fleming saving twice. To this point of his Ayr United career Fleming had faced ten penalties and had been beaten only once. This statistic excludes shootouts which are technically not penalties anyway because a penalty can only occur when an offence has been committed. The previous May he had three shootout saves against Stranraer in the promotion decider.

Arising from the night's events the big story was not about Greg Fleming nor even the Ayr United victory. The headlines were about Michael Rose making history as the fourth substitute.

Queen's Park 2 Ayr United 2 after extra time. Ayr United won the shootout 5-4. Scottish Cup fourth round replay.

Team: Fleming, Devlin, (Rose 120 + 1), Balatoni, Murphy, Boyle, Docherty, Crawford, Gilmour (Cairney 58), Donald (Forrest 71), Harkins and Moore (McGuffie 71); unused substitutes – Adams, McKenna and Hart.

Scorers: Craig Moore, Conrad Balatoni.

Shootout: Alan Forrest, Michael Rose, Craig McGuffie, Gary Harkins, Paddy Boyle

STEVO THE GOALIE

Ayr United versus Raith Rovers – 28th February, 2017

This was a Tuesday evening fixture and in the build-up there were some strange comments emanating from the direction of Kirkcaldy. If the comments were to be believed the three goalkeepers on Raith Rovers' books were all injured. Their manager at the time was John 'Yogi' Hughes who remains the only player to have led Ayr United out at a major cup final. Yogi was reputed for having a good sense of humour so it was quite conceivable that it was all a wind-up. Yet he was adamant that Kevin Cuthbert, Aaron Lennox and Conor Brennan were out of contention. A late request to postpone the fixture was refused. An SPFL statement read: "They could have brought in an under-21 goalkeeper or an out-of-contract goalkeeper of any age, in each case without any permission from the SPFL board. They could also have sought permission from the SPFL board to bring in a goalkeeper of any age on an emergency basis. All of these options were explained to Raith Rovers who chose to do none of these things and instead requested a postponement on the day of the match."

There was an historical precedent for this. Just short of 100 years earlier, on 21st April, 1917, Raith turned up at Somerset Park without a match fit goalkeeper. Although it was a league fixture Sprigger White, the Ayr United reserve goalkeeper, guested for them in a 2-1 home win. During the Great War such vagaries were common in football. No such contingencies could be made in 2017. While many of the fans were heading for the match it emerged that the visiting goalkeeper would be Ryan Stevenson. Not only was he a midfielder, he was an Ayr United legend. Stevo in an opposition shirt seemed unorthodox. The thought of him in an opposition goalkeeper's shirt was plain crazy. He had two spells at the club between which he played for Hearts, Ipswich Town and Partick Thistle. When his club was playing on a Sunday Stevo often took the opportunity to go and watch Ayr United, even as a standing spectator at the Somerset Road end. Would he be a standing spectator on this occasion or would he be in line for a busy shift? With both clubs in the Championship's relegation mire there was no scope for sentiment.

Stevenson had last played at Ayr on Christmas Eve at which time he was with Dumbarton. How well would he now stand scrutiny as a goalkeeper? Barely a minute had been played when he had an outstanding diving save from a Farid El Alagui header. He seemed to draw encouragement from his early success. Four minutes from half-time he had another outstanding save. This time it came from a Michael Rose drive which he managed to get down to. By half-time he had kept a clean goal and his team had the closest chance of the first half when a Ryan Hardie header struck the Ayr crossbar.

With the team now shooting towards the favoured Somerset Road end there was hope of making a breakthrough. It was little more than hope. With an hour played the stalemate had yet to be broken. In the 62nd minute Brian Gilmour played a short corner-kick to Alan Forrest who crossed for Farid El Alagui to score with a header at the back post. Beaten once, Stevo showed no sign of being beaten again. In stoppage time there was a scare when Jason Thomson went down in the Ayr box. Mercifully a goalkick was awarded.

At the start the whole issue had seemed farcical but the same could not be said of Ryan Stevenson's highly competent performance.

Ayr United 1 Raith Rovers 0. Championship.

Team: Fleming, Devlin, Gilmour, Forrest, Cairney (Rose 6), McGuffie (Boyle 84), McKenna, Wardrope (Moore 57), Meggatt, El Alagui and Balatoni; unused substitutes – Harkins, McKenzie and Hart.

Scorer: Farid El Alagui.

THE SLOPE

Beith Juniors versus Ayr United – 24ᵗʰ November, 2018

The laws of the game make provision for minimum and maximum pitch dimensions. This is deemed to be so important that it is dealt with under Law 1 which has the heading 'Field Of Play'. The requirements are laid out in forensic detail but nowhere is there any mention of gradient. The Easter Road slope was famous in Scottish football. It was removed when Hibs levelled the pitch in 2000. Less publicised sloping pitches were those at Glebe Park (Brechin) and Douglas Park (Hamilton).

A stir was created when Ayr United were drawn to play at Beith in the third round of the Scottish Cup. Most of our fans would have been barely aware that Beith Juniors were even in the draw. The prospect of playing an Ayrshire Junior club prompted conversations about it being a trip into the unknown. A few stories emerged. For example their manager was ex-Ayr United player John Millar and their goalkeeper was Stephen Grindlay, also a former Ayr United player. There was also a story that Bellsdale Park was on a slope. The tie was convenient for the author with in-laws living just walking distance from the ground. That was the parking and the pre-match cup of tea sorted out. Then it was time to become part of the all-ticket crowd of 1,780.

Beith was built on a hill so it was perfectly natural that the football ground was on a hill. Only on arrival at the ground did the true extent of the slope become apparent. The drop from one goal to the other was eight feet. An incline was expected but not on this scale. Eight feet! Bellsdale Park is a nice ground in a nice setting. The people running the club were most welcoming. Yet pre-match it did seem as if the gradient could have an influence on the tie. In retrospect it might logically have been argued that each team would have the advantage of the gradient for forty-five minutes.

Lawrence Shankland looked at ease on the contours.

Steven Bell won the toss and elected to play uphill in the first half. Normally the captain who wins the toss would elect to take any advantage in the first half. The rationale here is that a strong wind could drop in the second half. Steven Bell knew what he was doing. By the second half the slope would still be there!

Literally and metaphorically the first half was an uphill struggle. Stephen Grindlay was outstanding in goal for Beith and the breakthrough proved obstinately difficult. It took until the 64th minute to gain the lead. Michael Moffat sent in a cross which Steven Bell had difficulty in controlling due to the close attention of two Beith defenders but the ball broke to Lawrence Shankland who gleefully slammed it into the net – he just loved scoring! In the 79th minute Shankland was unmarked and he had ample space but elected to pass to Ross Docherty who applied a scoring finish. Two minutes from the end Luke McCowan delivered a dangerous ball into the box and Michael Moffat subtly dinked it into the net via the post.

The tie was emphatically won in the second half but we must draw the inescapable conclusion that by then we were playing downhill. In suggesting that Beith fought hard there is no patronising intent. Putting it into context was the result of our next match six days later – Dundee United 0 Ayr United 5. There was no mention of the word 'uphill' that night.

Beith Juniors 0 Ayr United 3. Scottish Cup third round.

Team: Doohan, Smith, Rose, Higgins, Harvie, McDaid (McCowan 84), Bell, Geggan (Docherty 73), Crawford (McGuffie 75), Moffat and Shankland; unused substitutes – Ecrepont, Ferguson, Murdoch and Hare-Reid.

Scorers: Lawrence Shankland, Ross Docherty and Michael Moffat.

Declan McDaid on the all too apparent slope

THE WALL HAS GONE

Ayr United versus Queen of the South – 9th April, 2019

On a pleasant Tuesday evening a home win was sought in order to regain third place in the Championship. However when the fans entered the ground there was a major distraction. At the Railway End there was no boundary wall. It had been there at the home match against Inverness Caledonian Thistle on the Saturday. This was merely three days before. It had stood there since the summer of 1950. In May 1950 an appeal was made for volunteer bricklayers and plasters to construct a wall round the track at Somerset Park. This was co-ordinated by the Ayr United Supporters' Association. A buy-a-brick campaign got launched. The cost was a shilling a brick. This work was not merely cosmetic. The original wooden fencing had rotted and had gradually fallen away. There was a good response to the appeal for volunteer labour. It was toil, sweat, camaraderie and copious amounts of tea laid on. Skill was a factor too. Let us not forget that bricklaying is a craft. Dismantling the old wooden fencing in 1950 was the easy part. It was falling away already. Dismantling the 1950 wall in 2019 was an entirely different prospect and it spoke volumes for the quality of the craftsmanship all these years ago.

The demolition at the Railway End was just the start of the work. When the fans next returned to Somerset Park it was noticed that the walls had been demolished and replaced around the entire track. The question may be asked as to why a solid wall had to be replaced. The answer is that it was done at the behest of South Ayrshire Council. Expanding the answer in any greater detail would be a sleep-inducing experience relating to a series of technical reports and regulations.

The only goal in the Queen of the South match came at the then un-walled end. Josh Todd committed a handling offence. Mark Kerr took the resultant free-kick and it was met by Steven Bell who headed it back to Robbie Crawford who was immediately hauled down by Todd. Lawrence Shankland beat Jack Leighfield from the spot with the ball entering the net via the underside of the crossbar. This was just two minutes before half-time and it was enough to regain third place.

The volunteers of 1950 having a well earned break during construction of the boundary wall. Visible at their feet is the old fencing

Before departing this tale it is worth mentioning that the volunteer tradesmen of 1950 did not rest on their laurels. They constructed a gymnasium at the top of Tryfield Place and it was formally opened on 13th March, 1952. Then, in 1954, a most ambitious project was tackled. This was the retaining wall between Somerset Park and WG Walker's. The minute book of the Supporters' Association contained this entry.

"The general secretary reported having met some of the directors of Ayr United Football Club and he had the ground marked off for the retaining wall between the ground and Messrs Walker's and stated that works had commenced on 9/5/54, excavation would start on 16/5/54 and building on 23/5/54. The chairman hoped that members would turn up to assist. A building committee was formed on the motion of Mr J. Faber, seconded by Mr A. Anderson, the committee to consist of Messrs Burt, White, McKenna, Main, Stirrat and Boyle, Messrs White and McKenna to be joint convenors and Mr Burt agreed to supervise return of all working tools at the end of each working period. The purchase of barrows was moved by Mr A. Main and seconded by Mr Faber. A motion that we limit expenditure on building to £400 was agreed to without a division."

Ayr United 1 Queen of the South 0. Championship.
Team: Doohan, Smith, Bell, Rose, Harvie, Geggan (Murdoch 70), Kerr, Crawford, Cadden (McDaid 61), Shankland and Miller (Moore 77); unused substitutes – Moffat, Forrest, Docherty, Hare-Reid.
Scorer: Lawrence Shankland.

Can we have our wall back, please?

Lightning Source UK Ltd.
Milton Keynes UK
UKHW021018201220
375517UK00011B/2574